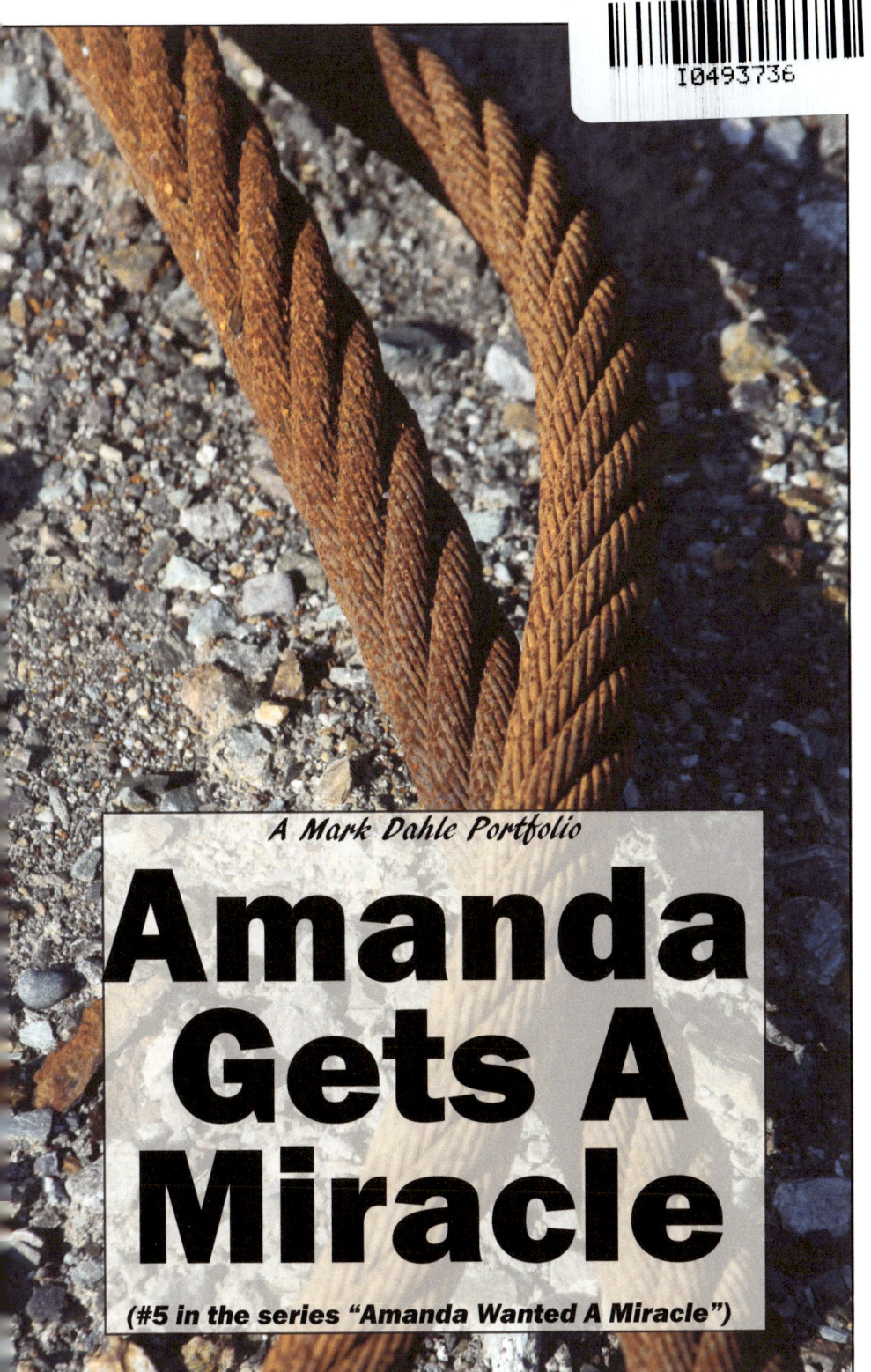

A Mark Dahle Portfolio

Amanda Gets A Miracle

(#5 in the series "Amanda Wanted A Miracle")

This is the fifth story about Amanda.
The books in this series:

~ ~ ~

Mark Dahle Portfolios can be read in a few minutes and enjoyed for a lifetime.

Unlike many picture books, the text in this book is not related to the art. This might seem weird at first. One thing that makes it better is to order more portfolios until you get used to it. Fortunately, space is provided on the pages for you to draw your own pictures of Amanda if you like.

This portfolio includes a beautiful 36 x 24 inch painting (at the right), twenty-nine great photos from Ketchikan, Alaska, and a story about Amanda, who (finally!) got the miracle she wanted.

Photographs in this book are available in limited editions. See http://www.MarkDahle.com for more information and for previews of upcoming portfolios.

We do our best to create portfolios free of editing mistakes. But if we miss anything, we reward people who report errors. For details see MarkDahle.com/Typos.html or email MarkDahle@aol.com with the subject line "Typos." Thanks!

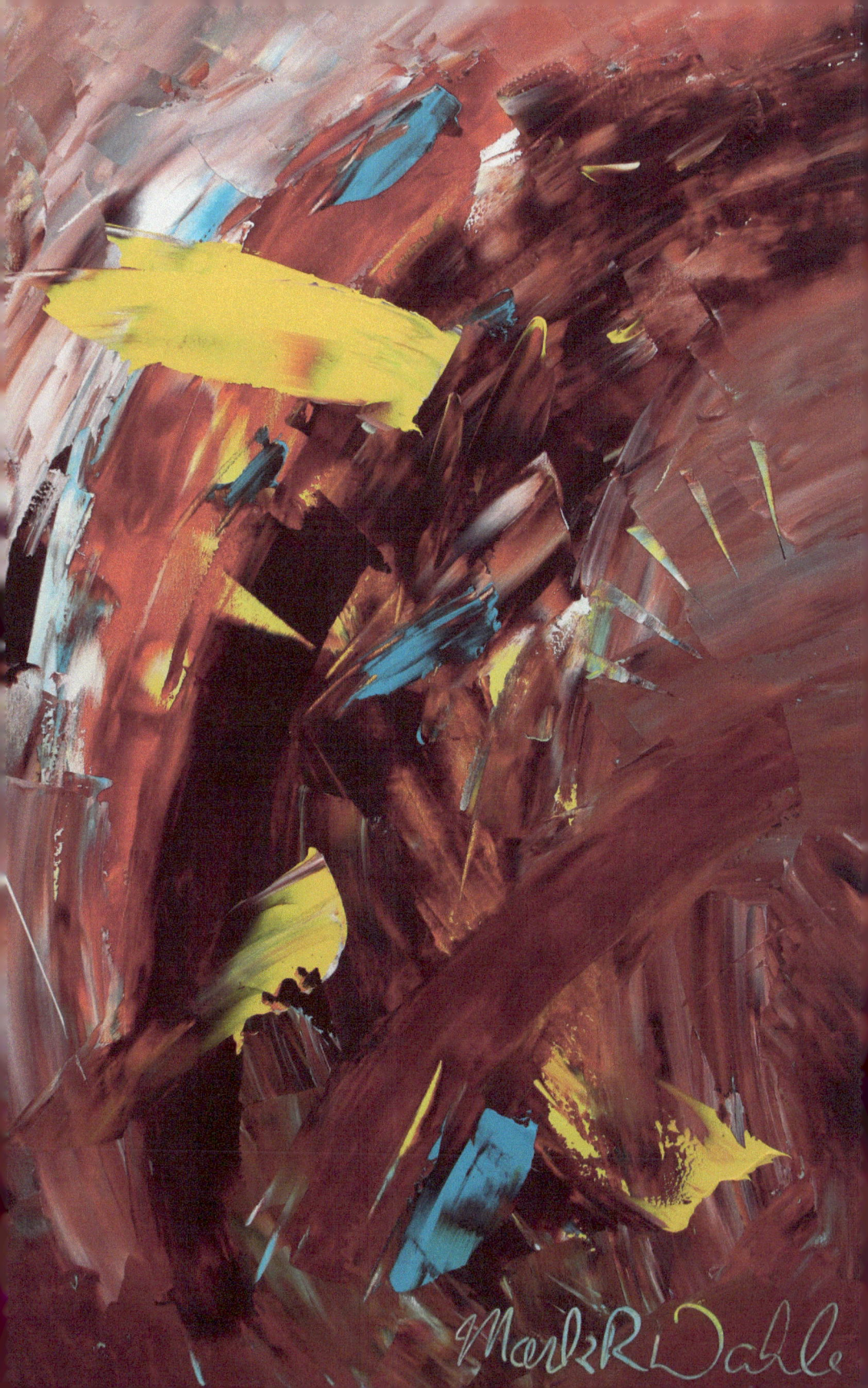

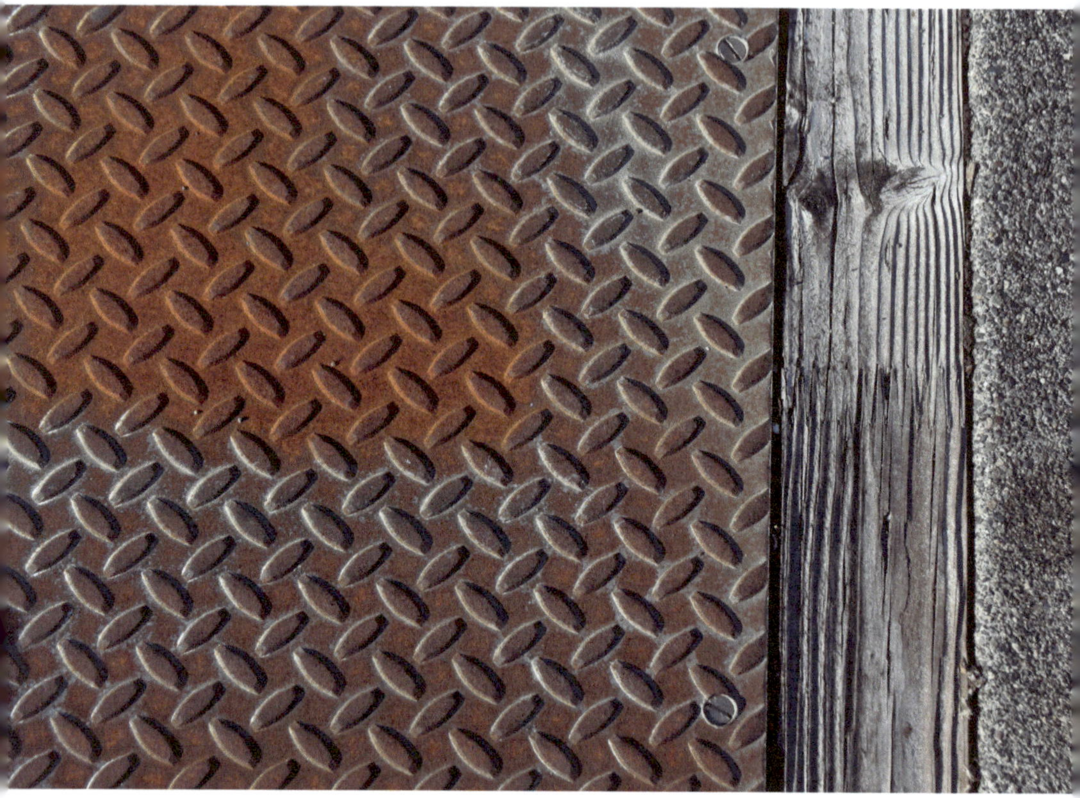

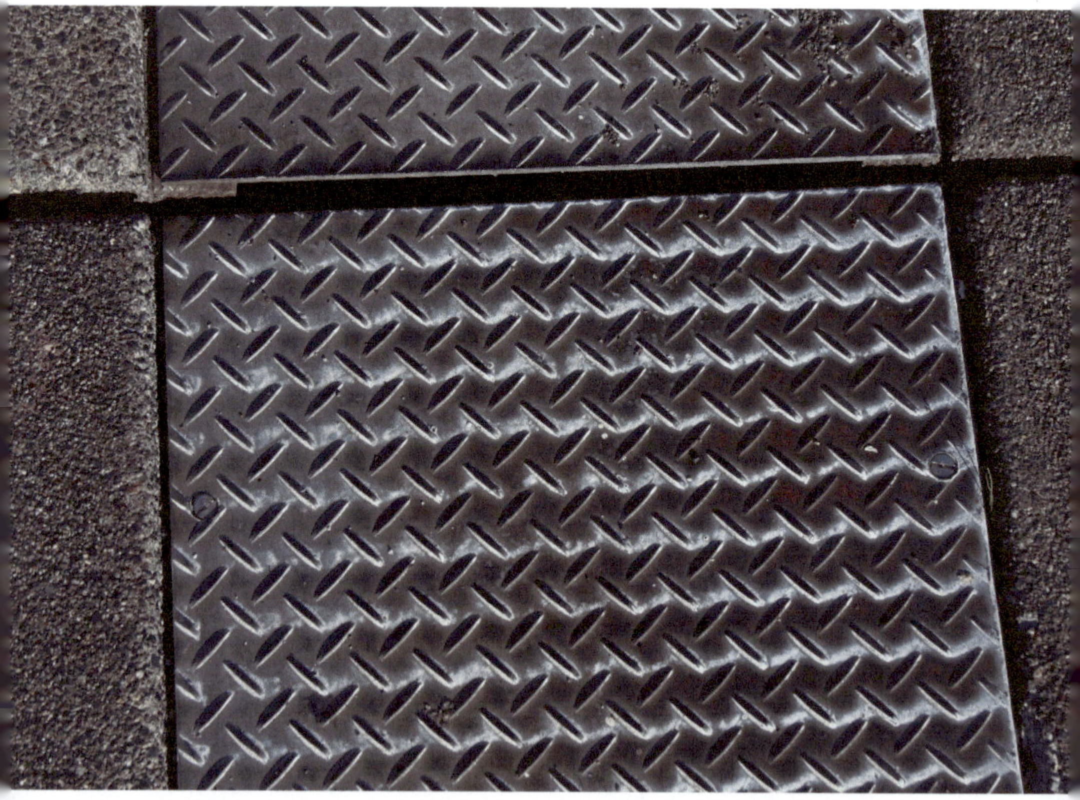

Amanda's mom had no intention of leaving her home just because a couple neighbors were upset and had chopped up Amanda's garden. She had spent a good part of her life trying to get away from the influence of her father (and her mother, too), and she wasn't going to let a few angry neighbors push her back to her father's house. She would watch his house for him if he wasn't there. But if he *was* there? She wasn't going back.

That night a fire started on the fence near Amanda's plants. A wind was howling, and before anyone noticed, the fence was ablaze and the wind was blowing the fire toward the house.

Amanda woke in the middle of the night to see the most delightful patterns of light flickering on the ceiling of her room. It was the most curious thing she had seen yet. She watched the patterns on the ceiling for a few seconds, then got up to look out the window to see what could cause such a beautiful thing. Her room was on the second floor, and she had a clear view of the fence ablaze, with the flames getting closer and closer to the house.

"Fire!" she yelled. "The fence is on fire! Mom! The fence is on fire!"

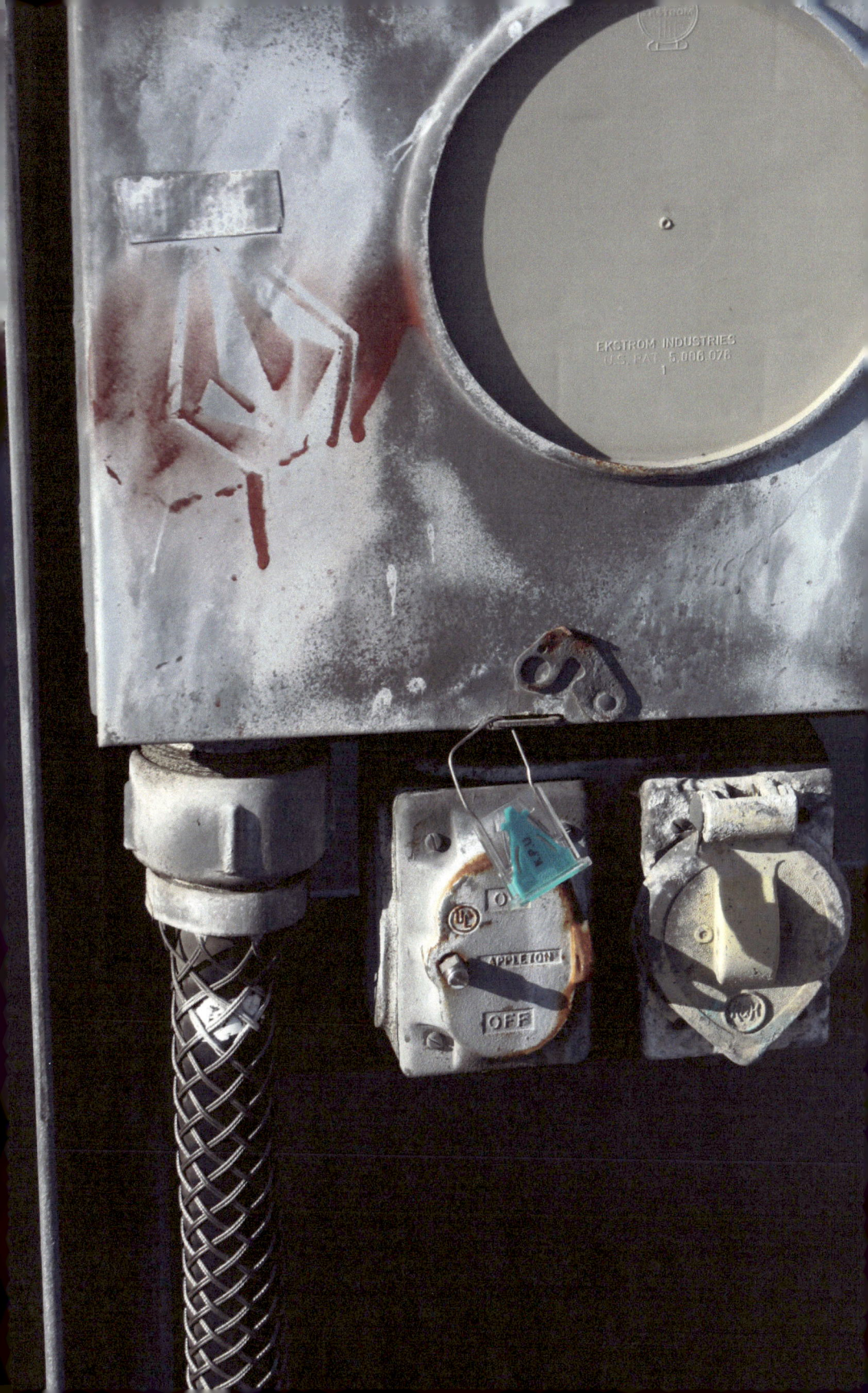

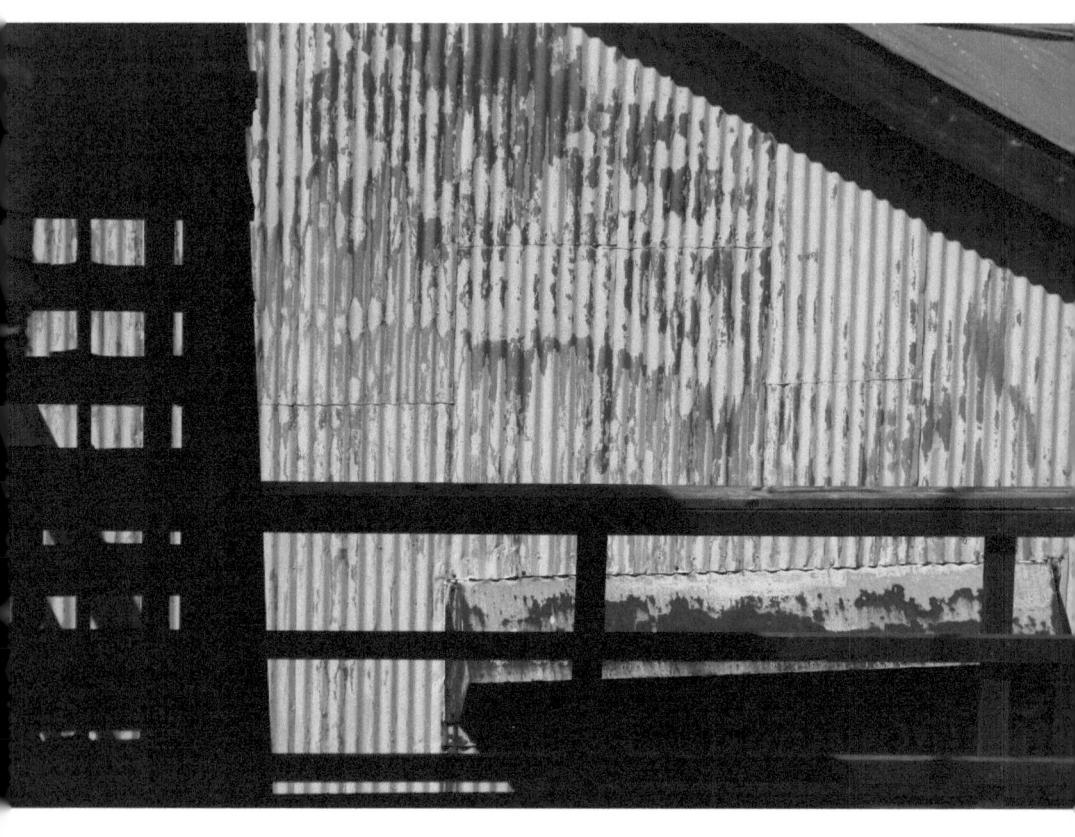

Her mother had been sleeping soundly, but she awoke with a start. Her room, right below Amanda's, had double glass doors leading onto the patio, and when she opened the curtains she had a full view of the flames.

"Amanda!" she yelled. "Call 911! Tell them we have a fire. Then grab some clothes. We have to get out. I'm going to get your brother."

Amanda's mom quickly filled a suitcase with clothes for herself and Amanda's brother. She grabbed a photo of their family, taken six years earlier, before her son was born but when Amanda's dad was still living. She grabbed her wallet and checkbook and a packet of documents she kept in case of emergencies.

Then she scooped up her still sleeping son and called to Amanda.

"Amanda! Did you call 911 yet? We have to leave *now!*"

Amanda had not called. She had been staring out her window at the fire, watching it advance down the fence toward the house, watching the hypnotic colors and thinking about her smashed plants near where the flames had started.

"Amanda!" The urgent call shook Amanda out of her trance. Then suddenly her mom was at the door to her room, carrying her brother. "Amanda! Did you call 911?"

"Not yet."

"Did you get your clothes?"

Amanda gave a helpless shrug. "Will the fire kill my plants?" she asked.

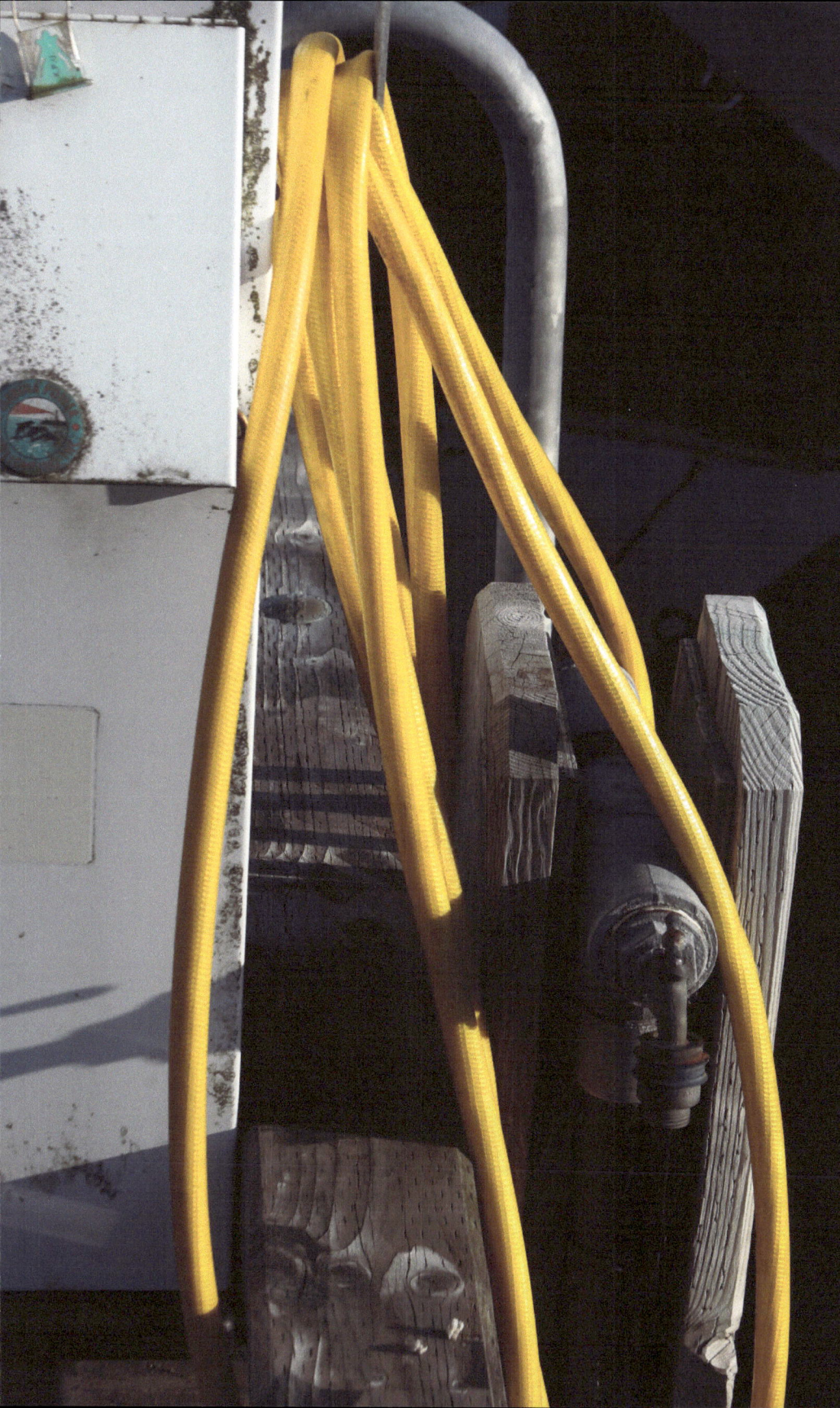

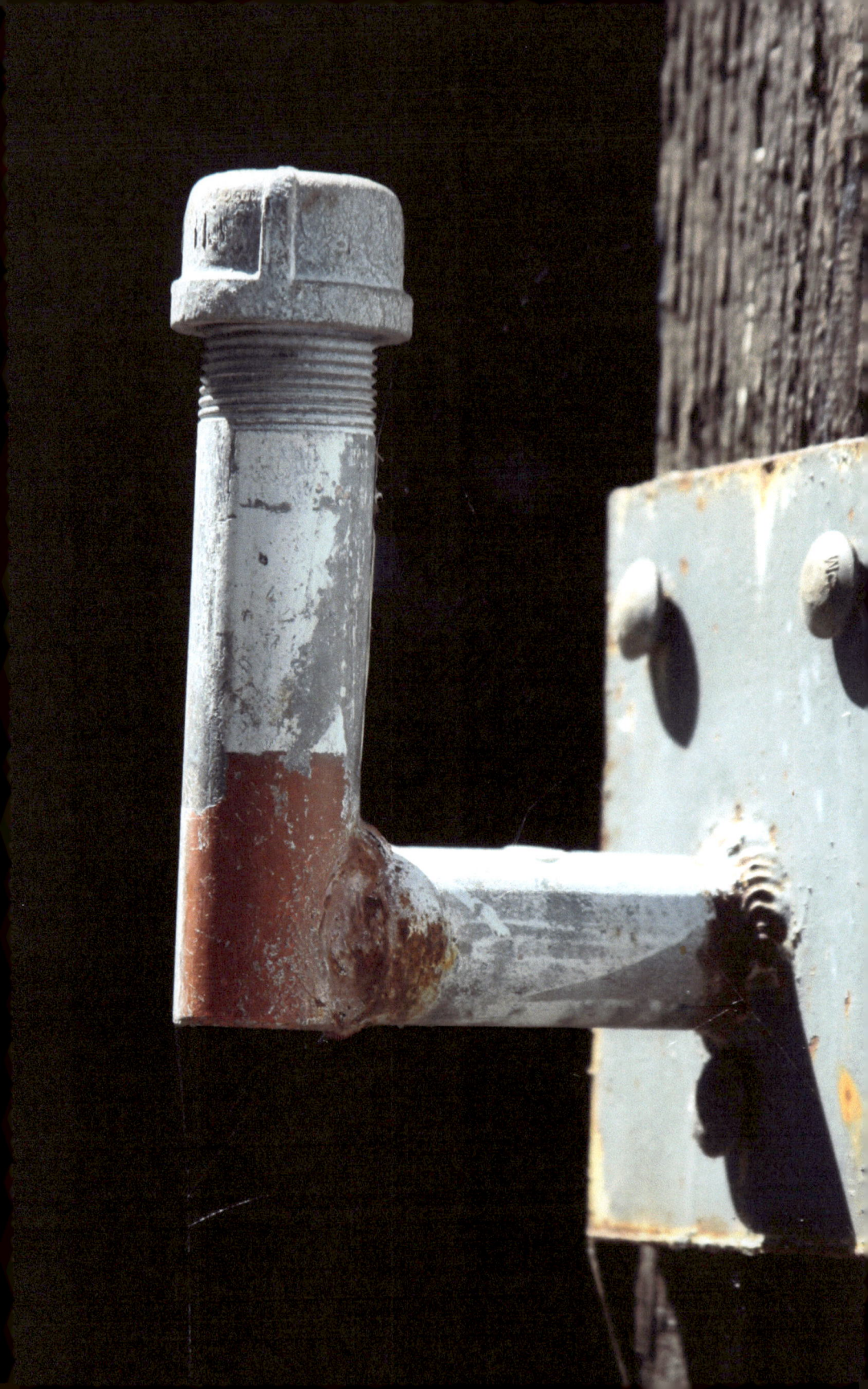

Amanda's mom looked at her daughter, first with shock, then with compassion. "I don't know, Amanda. But listen: We have to leave *right now*. We'll talk about your plants later. Take your brother's hand and both of you go out the front door and stand by the car."

Amanda's mom grabbed a phone, called 911, and reported the blaze while she hurriedly scooped up some clothes for Amanda. At the last minute she remembered Amanda's stuffed bear. Then she grabbed the suitcase she had filled with her own clothes and documents and raced out the front door just as the flames reached the back porch.

All three got in the car. Amanda's mom drove a short distance, did a U-turn, then pulled over to the curb at a spot where they could watch the house in safety. The flames were over the roof before the fire department arrived. By the time the hoses were in place, the fire had engulfed the back half of the house.

They stayed in the car, watching the fire department battle the blaze. But the winds were so fierce and the fire had such an early start that the fire department mostly just tried to keep the other houses in the neighborhood from burning. Amanda and her mom and brother watched for long stretches in complete silence.

When it was over, the house was a total loss. The front was still standing. But the back of the house was completely burned and anything inside that hadn't burned was ruined by all the water poured on the blaze.

"Well," said Amanda's mom when they surveyed the damage late that afternoon, "I guess we're going to visit your grandfather after all."

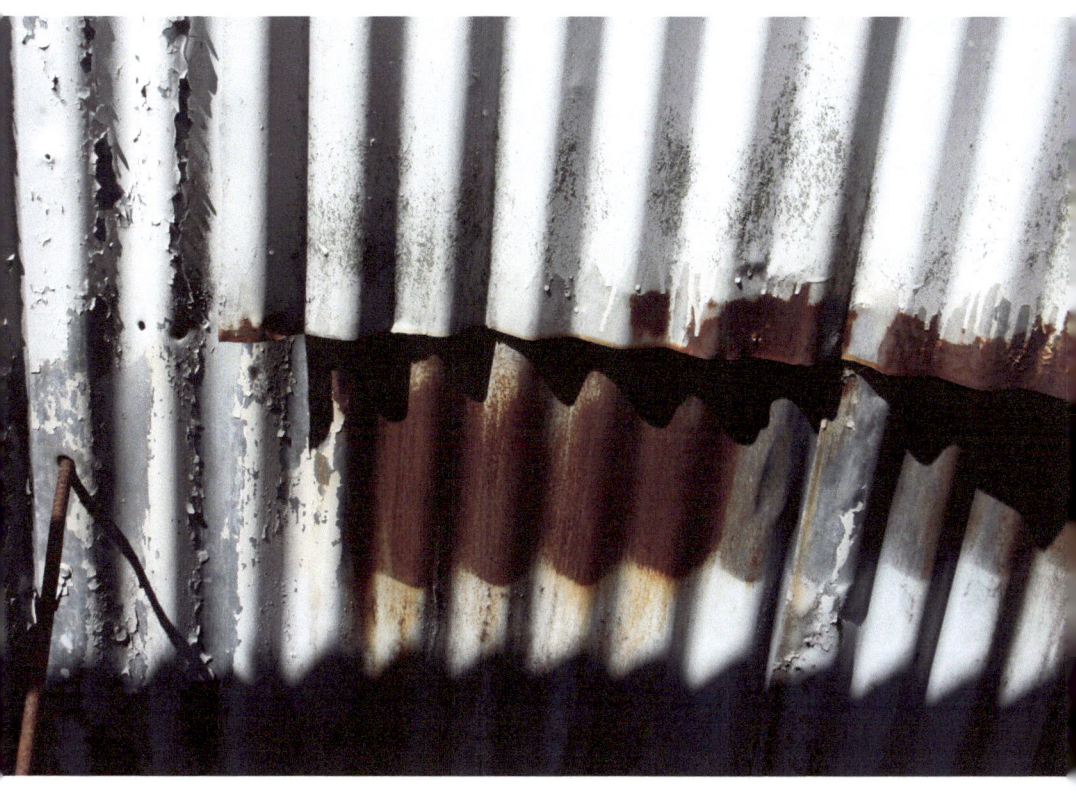

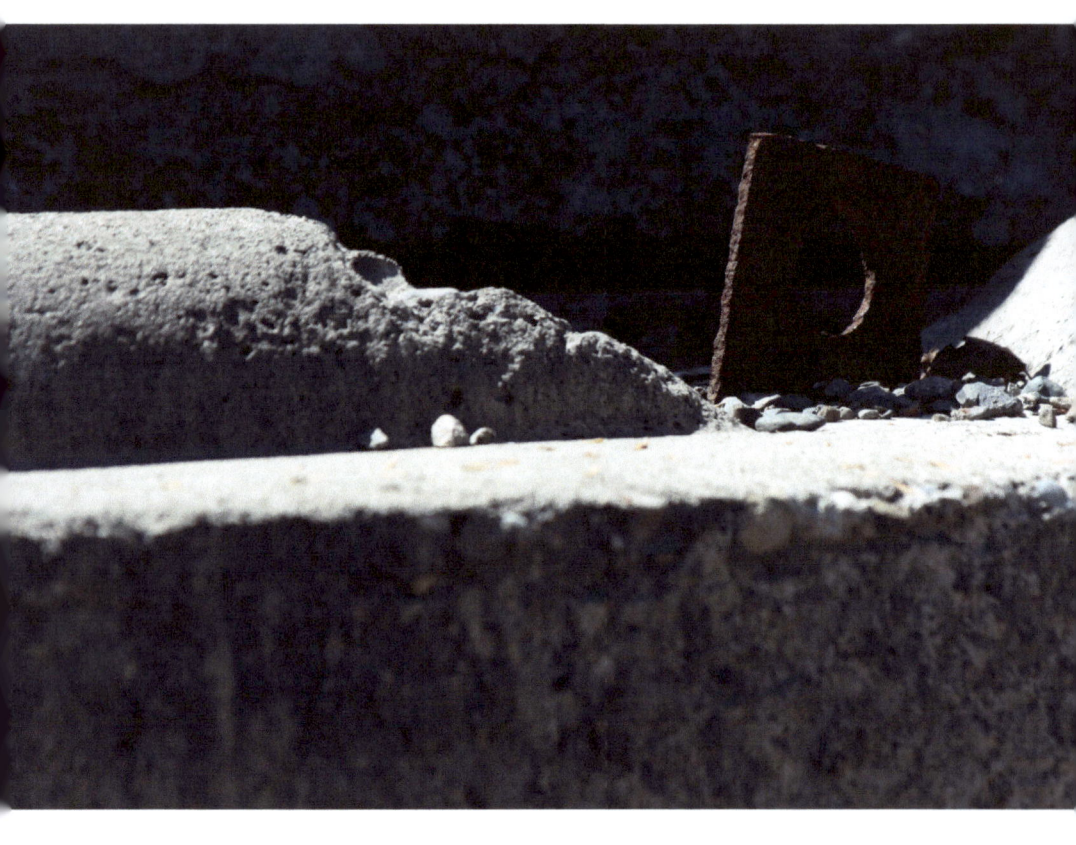

When Amanda learned that her stuffed bear had survived the fire, the only other thing she wondered about was her plants. At the end of the day they got permission to go back to her garden to look.

Amanda and her mom and brother walked past a few smoldering sticks where the fence used to be.

When they got to the garden, they found the spot where Amanda's neighbor had smashed all Amanda's plants and porcelain figures the day before. They were surprised to see that in four or five spots new shoots were already coming out of the ground from the bits of smashed plants. One of the shoots even had a fragrant flower ready to blossom. But all the plants were from seeds that Amanda's grandfather had given her. Nothing remained from the large seeds that Amanda had hoped would bring her miracle.

Amanda dug up four of the shoots and put them in a box so she could take them to her grandfather's. She left the shoot that already had a flower. It looked like it might have enough of a start to make it without being watered by Amanda every day.

That night they stayed at a motel, and the next day they drove to Amanda's grandfather's house. By then they had convinced Amanda's grandmother to come along with them, and the long drive was quite a bit more lively since she was in the car.

When they arrived that night, Amanda's grandfather greeted them at the door and showed each of them their rooms. Amanda got a nice room all her own at the top of the stairs. After she put her few clothes away, Amanda took the shoots to her grandfather.

"Do you think they'll grow here?" she asked.

"I'm certain of it," he said. "I know it's late, but I want you and your grandmother to see how well your plant is doing in my garden – it's full of blossoms even though it's surrounded by pumpkins and watermelons. I've never seen anything like it."

They all trooped out to the garden with flashlights. Even Amanda's brother came for a look.

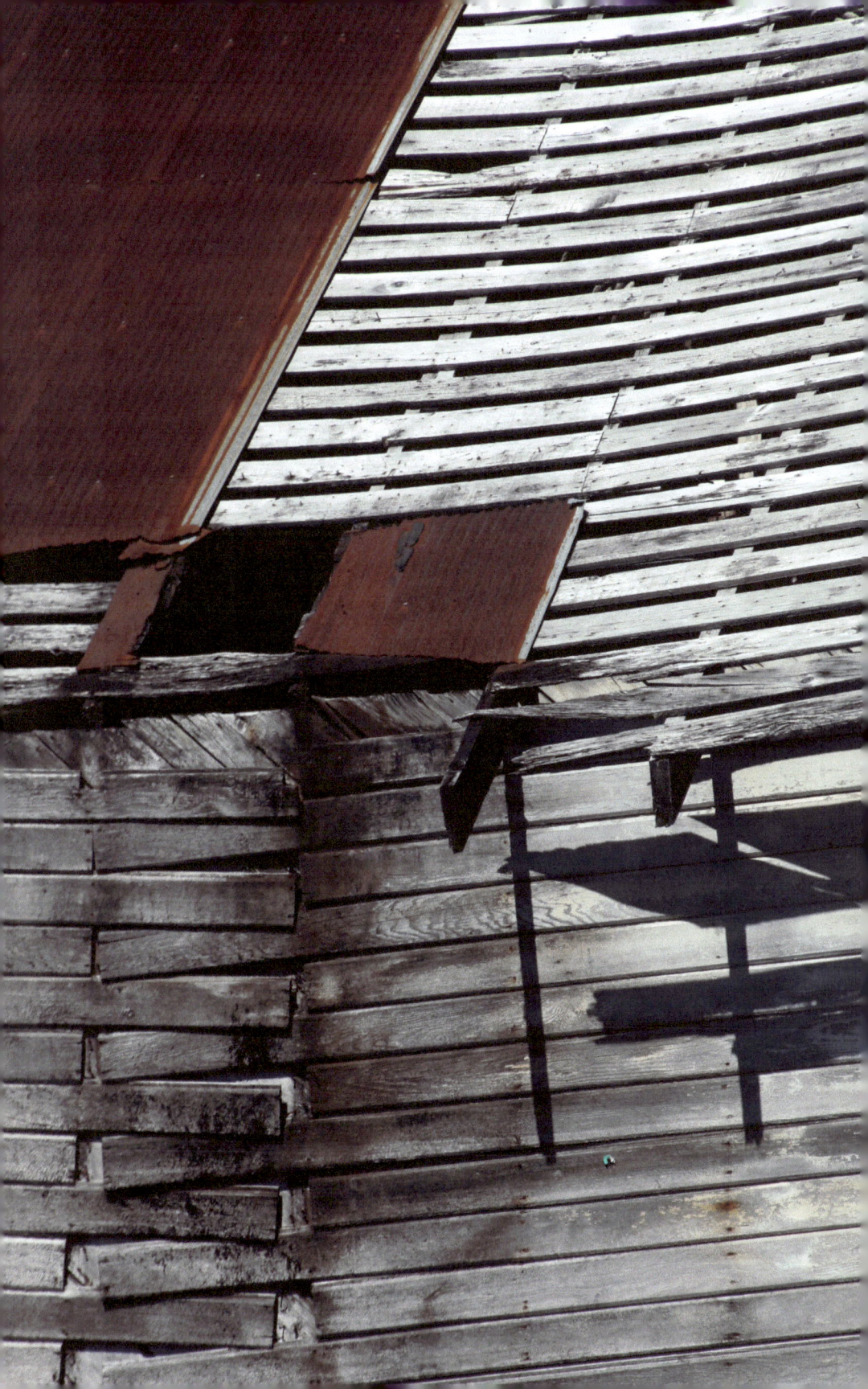

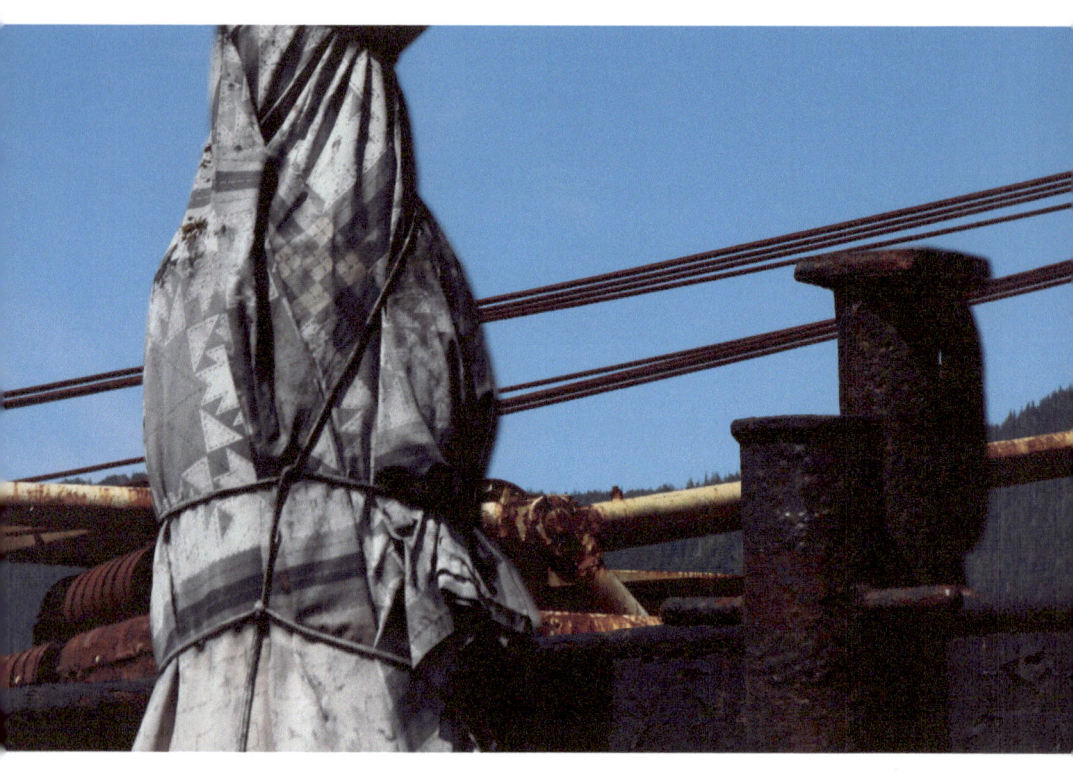

Amanda could smell the flowers long before she could see them. But she gasped when she finally got close. The plant that had been drooping so badly when she last saw it had fully recovered, and it was far more beautiful and colorful than she had imagined it would be.

"I can't believe it's doing so well next to those pumpkins," said her grandmother.

"And I can't believe it's doing so well next to the watermelons," said her grandfather. "I think it's because of the porcelain mouse Amanda gave me. The plant's been doing great ever since I put the two together."

Amanda's mom *hated* it when her parents talked like this. As if a porcelain mouse would make any difference to a plant. But she didn't say what she was thinking since Amanda was present.

"I think the shoots you brought should go near this plant," said Amanda's grandfather. "I'd have gotten the soil ready myself, but it will be better for you if you do it."

So they all watched while Amanda dug up the soil and got it ready. Then she put the four shoots in the ground, far enough apart so they could each grow if they all survived.

When she was done, her grandparents, mom and brother all walked back to the house. Amanda stayed behind just long enough to pull some porcelain animals out of the air. This time she found a raccoon, a skunk, a fox and a weasel. Each were exceptionally beautiful, and she put one of them next to each of the shoots she had just planted.

She was ready to go back to the house when, on a whim, she reached into the air one more time and to her excitement and delight, caught hold of something that felt like pumpkin glop. She pulled with all her might, and managed to pull some out of the air. She was holding what looked like the mushy part inside a pumpkin, except it was green and the seed in the middle of it was enormous, close to two inches long.

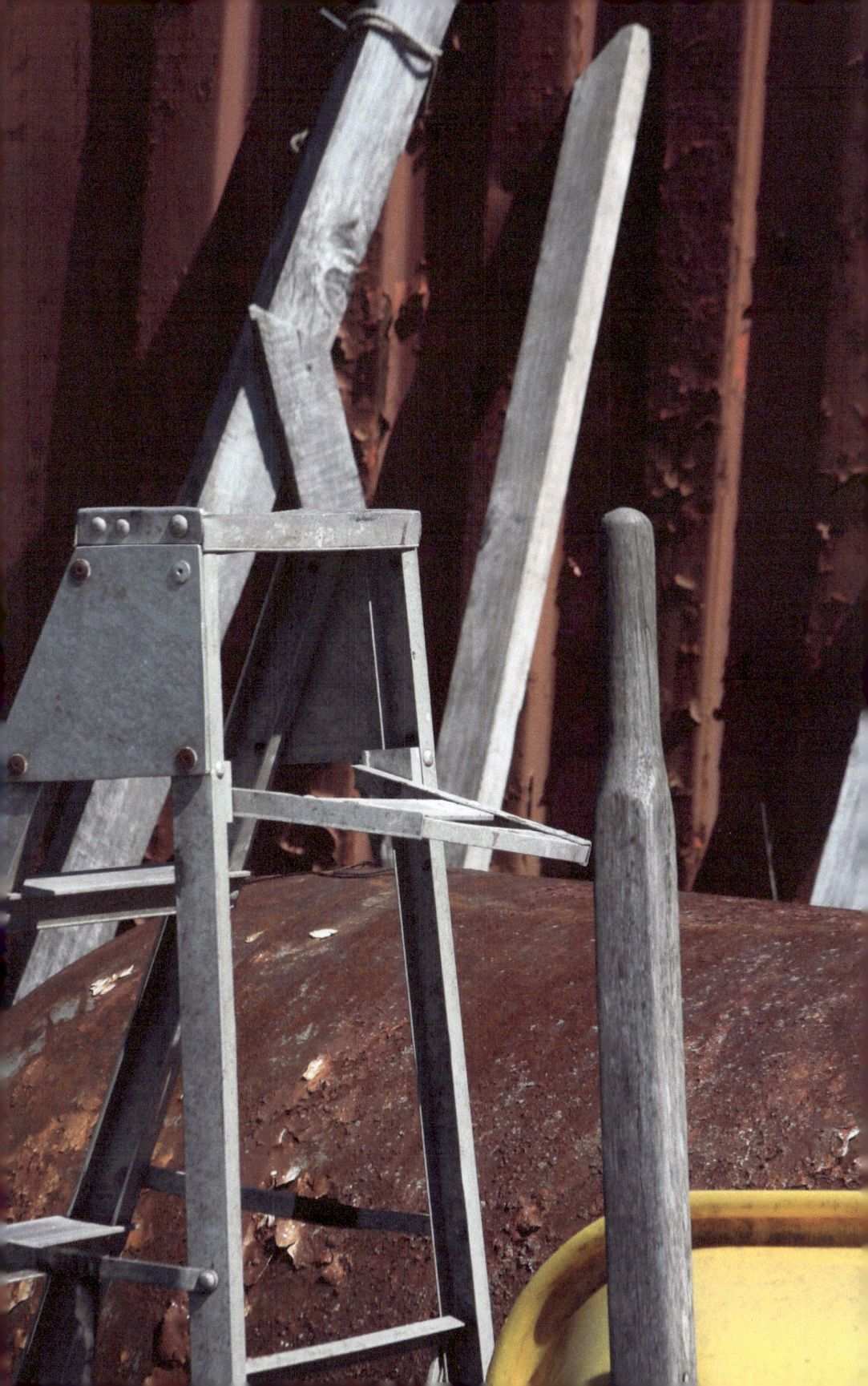

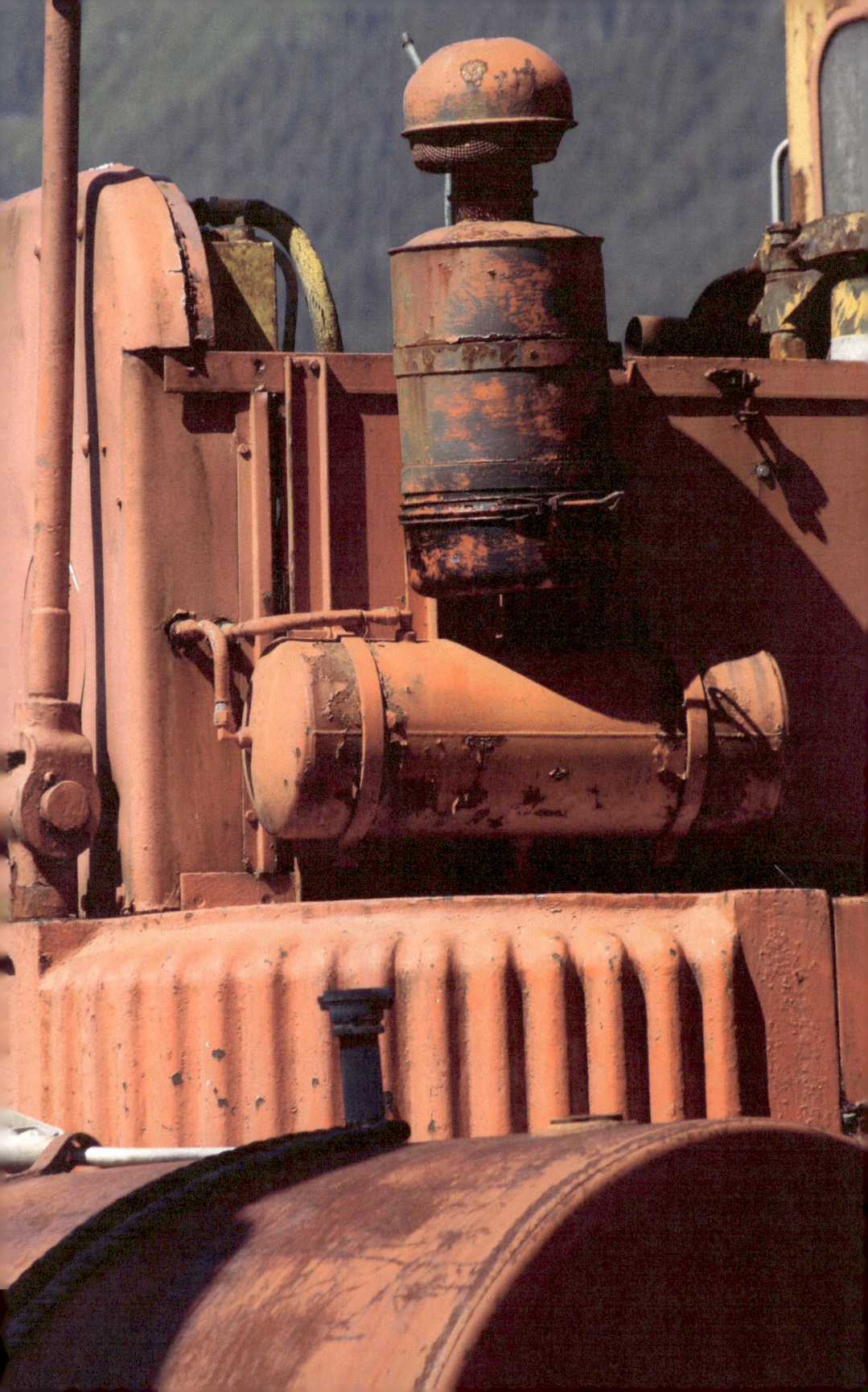

Amanda carefully buried the seed in the center of the four shoots. Then she reached into the air for a porcelain animal to place next to it. To her surprise, she didn't find an animal this time, but a beautiful wooden bridge with a rainbow shining over it. It was the most wonderful porcelain sculpture she had ever seen. She didn't know if she should bring it into the house or leave it in the garden, but she placed it near where she had buried the new seed. She looked at her work one last time, then ran to the house to be with the others.

For the rest of the evening, Amanda was smiling. She didn't know how, but she was certain she was going to get her miracle.

That night, after Amanda had gone to bed, Amanda heard her mom and her grandparents talking. Amanda decided to get out of bed and get some water. That's how she had found out that her grandmother pulled pumpkins out of the air. Maybe she'd learn something just as wonderful this time.

Amanda carefully crept down the stairs without making a sound and stood just outside the kitchen door so she could listen.

"I don't understand it," Amanda's mom was saying. "Amanda is normally so dependable. If she'd called 911 when I asked her to, we might have been able to save some of the house."

"How much later did *you* call?" asked Amanda's grandmother.

"At least a minute. Maybe two."

"Well," said her grandfather. "I'm really sorry you lost the house. But I don't think a minute or two would have made any difference."

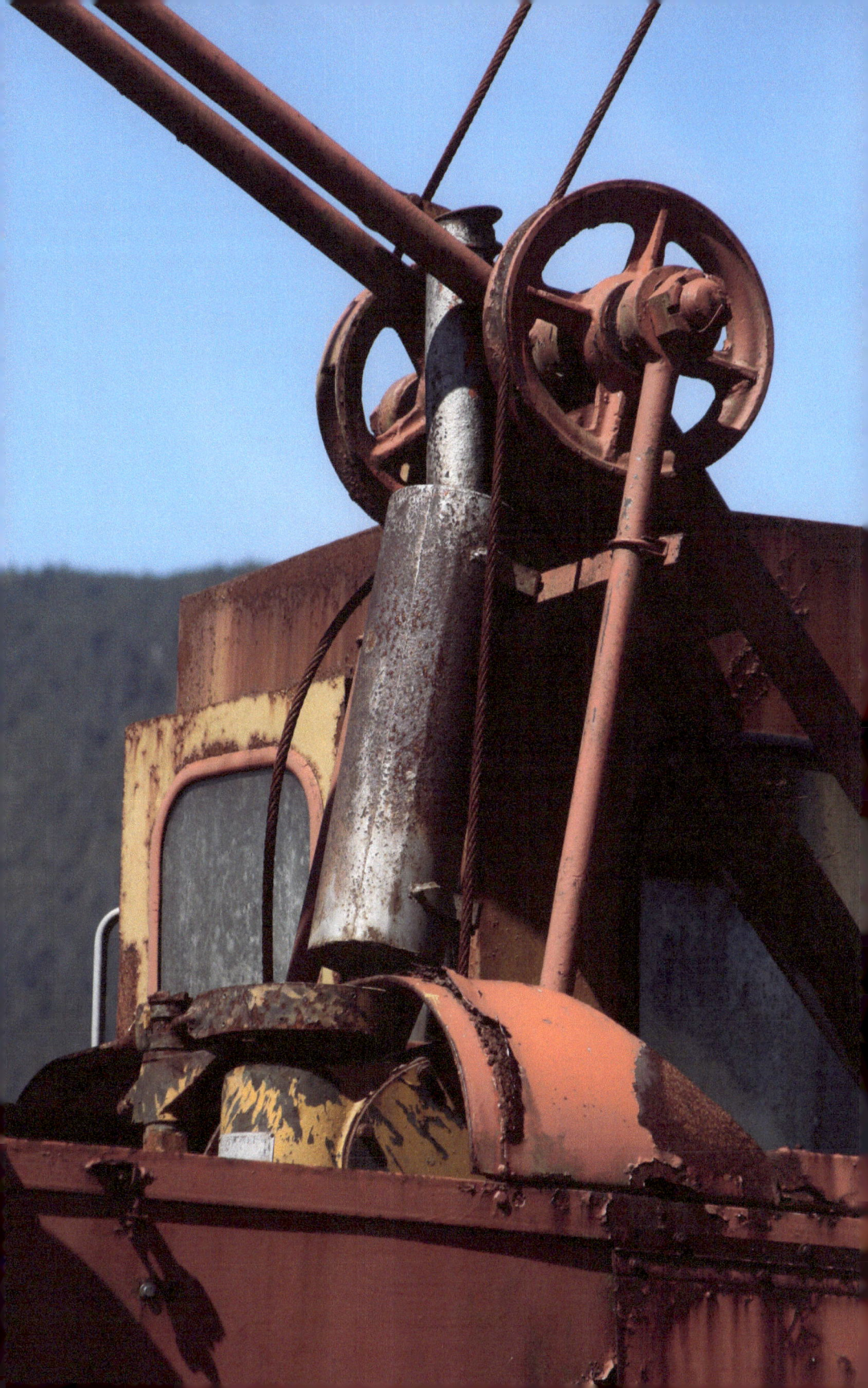

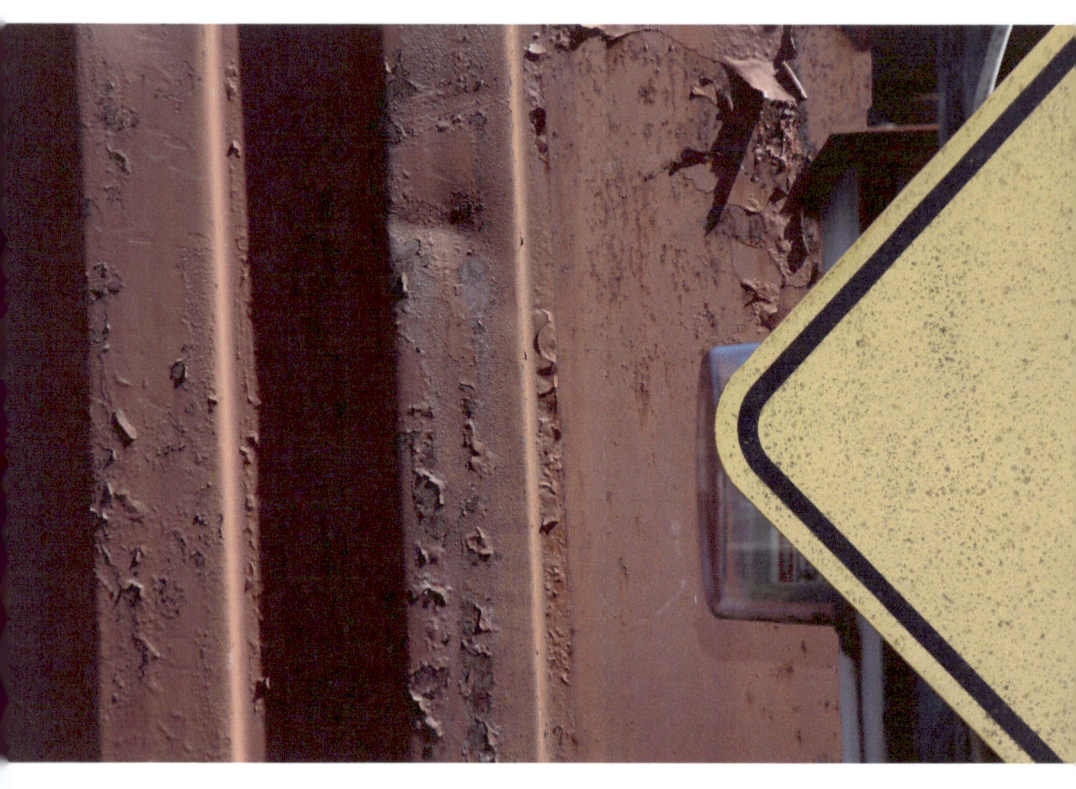

"Anyway, we're here, now," said her mom. "And I don't mean to be ungrateful, but you mustn't kid Amanda about things like that porcelain mouse helping the garden. She'll believe you, you know."

Amanda's grandfather was silent for a bit. "There was a time," he said, "when I didn't value pumpkins." He looked directly at Amanda's grandmother. "I'm sorry about that. Over the years, I've learned how important they are."

Then he continued, focusing again on Amanda's mom. "When I first saw the porcelain mouse, I thought it was nice that Amanda had given it to me. But I didn't think it would be useful. For years I've tried planting seeds in that patch of garden where Amanda's plant is growing. I've planted seeds just like what Amanda planted there. And I've never had *one* make it. The spot is too close to the watermelons and too close to the pumpkins.

"Amanda's plant was dying, just like all the others I've planted there over the years. I put the mouse beside it on a whim. It was Amanda's plant and Amanda's mouse, so I put them together. The plant started to recover that day. It's the first plant that's ever survived in that patch in more than twenty years. I really *do* think Amanda's mouse made a difference."

"Oh dad," said Amanda's mom. "You know I love you. But you mustn't say such things, even if you *do* believe them. At least not around Amanda. She'll think you're telling the truth."

There was silence for a while, but Amanda had heard enough. She began silently sneaking back up the stairs to her room. Her happiness was gone.

Did her mom really think it was Amanda's fault that the house burned as much as it did?

And what about the porcelain mouse? Earlier in the week, Amanda had believed her grandfather when he said the mouse had made a difference. That's why she put the porcelain figures around the shoots. But did they really matter? Her mom didn't seem to think so. And the figurines she had put in her garden at home hadn't kept the plants safe from the neighbors.

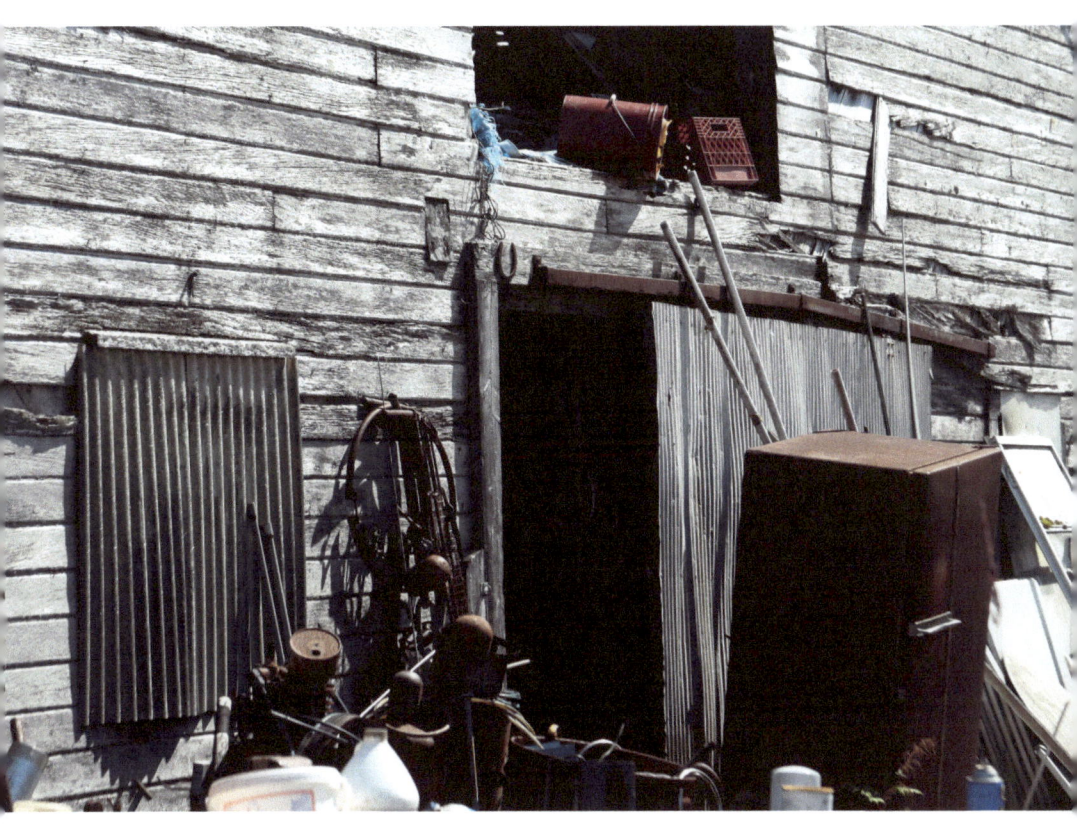

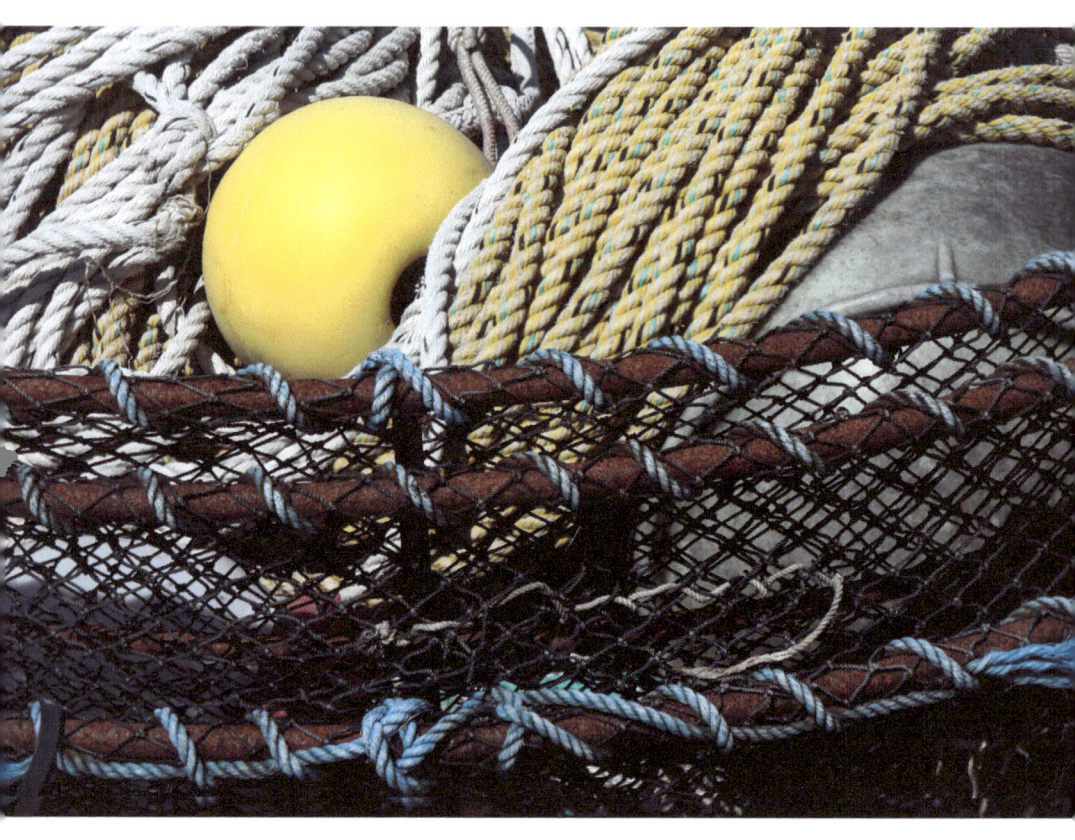

That night Amanda's dreams were not pleasant. She dreamed the beautiful plant in her garden at home lit a match and started the fire that burned the fence and burned the house. The plant was laughing at her. Then the plant took off a mask and she could see it was her angry neighbor with the big nose. He was pointing to her burned house and laughing and laughing and laughing. When Amanda woke up she was shaking. She didn't know what to think.

Normally on waking Amanda would have raced to the garden to see how her plants were doing. Now she wasn't sure she wanted to know. Did her plants really cause the fire that burned her house?

Amanda helped out with chores that morning. Then she went to a store with her mom to get new clothes.

The clothes they found were not wonderful.

"They're better than nothing," said her mom. "They'll do for a while."

That was little comfort to Amanda. She didn't like her new clothes. But mostly she was upset because she was worried about her plants. Would they hurt her grandfather's house, too? What if they lit another fire?

By the time Amanda got back with her ugly new clothes, Amanda was ready to yank all her plants out of the garden before they hurt someone else.

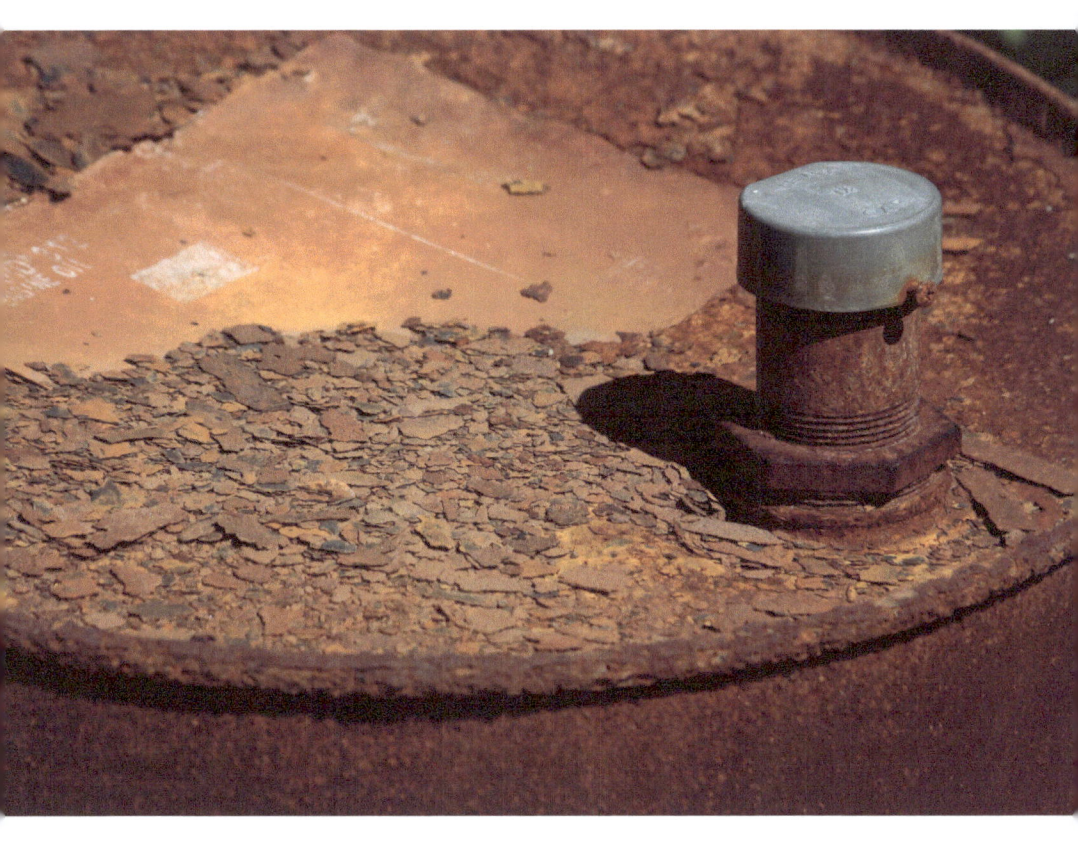

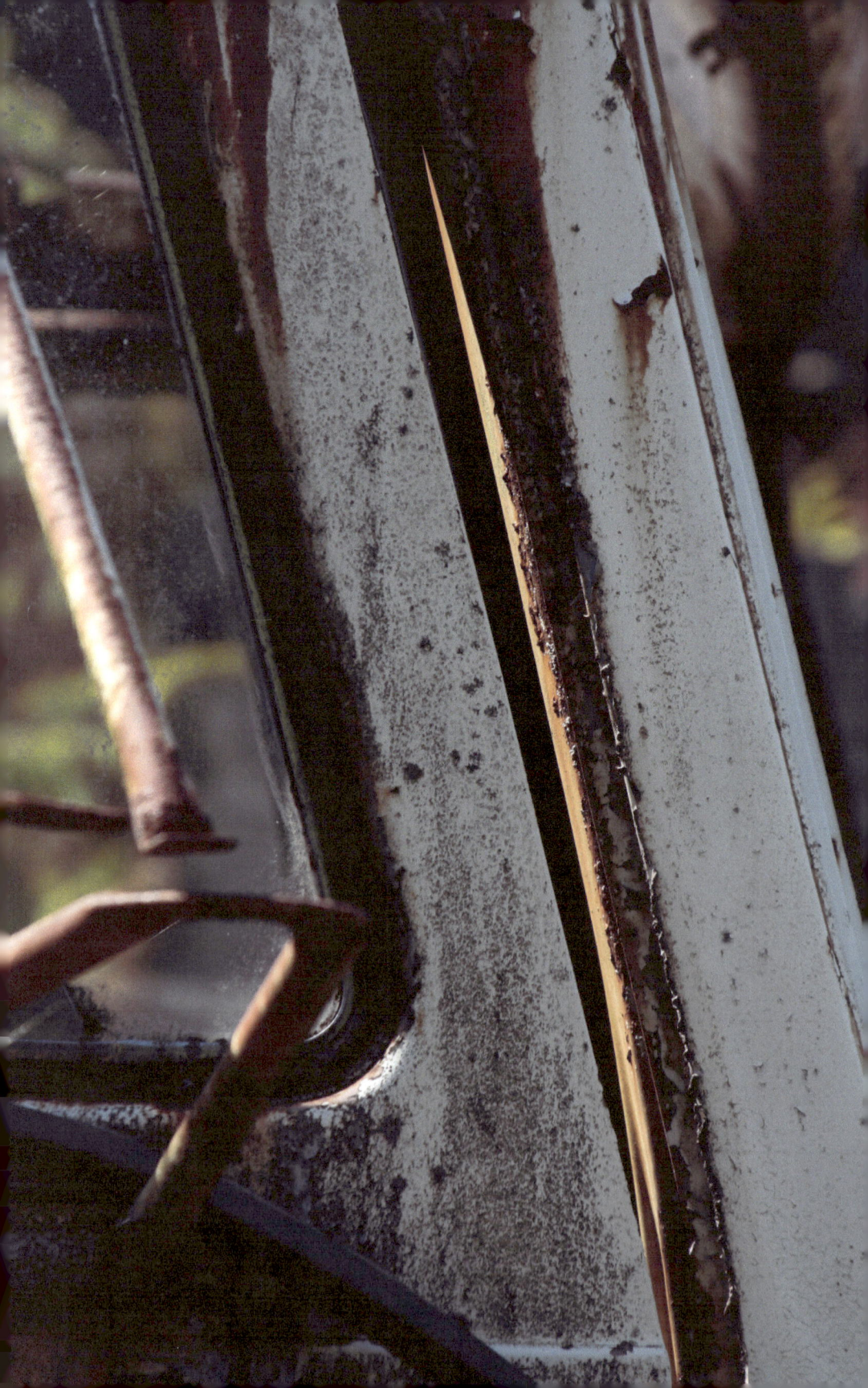

Luckily her grandmother met her at the car when she got back.

"Let me see what you got," she said. She admired Amanda's brother's clothes. Then she admired Amanda's clothes. She helped put the clothes in the closets in their rooms. Then she took Amanda's hand. "Amanda and I are going for a walk," she said. "We'll be gone for a while."

She took Amanda out to the garden. Half way between the pumpkins and the watermelons she had already set out three chairs. She and Amanda each sat in one.

"Is someone else coming?" Amanda asked.

"You never know," said her grandmother. "But even if no one else comes, I want to talk with you. I recognize that look in your eyes."

"What look?" asked Amanda.

"The look that comes when you're wondering if you should tear your plants out of the garden."

Amanda looked at her grandmother's face, startled. How did she know *that*?

"I know that look because I felt it myself years ago. And *my* grandmother sat me down to talk, just like I'm doing."

Amanda's grandmother poured some lemonade that was on a nearby table and gave Amanda and herself a glass.

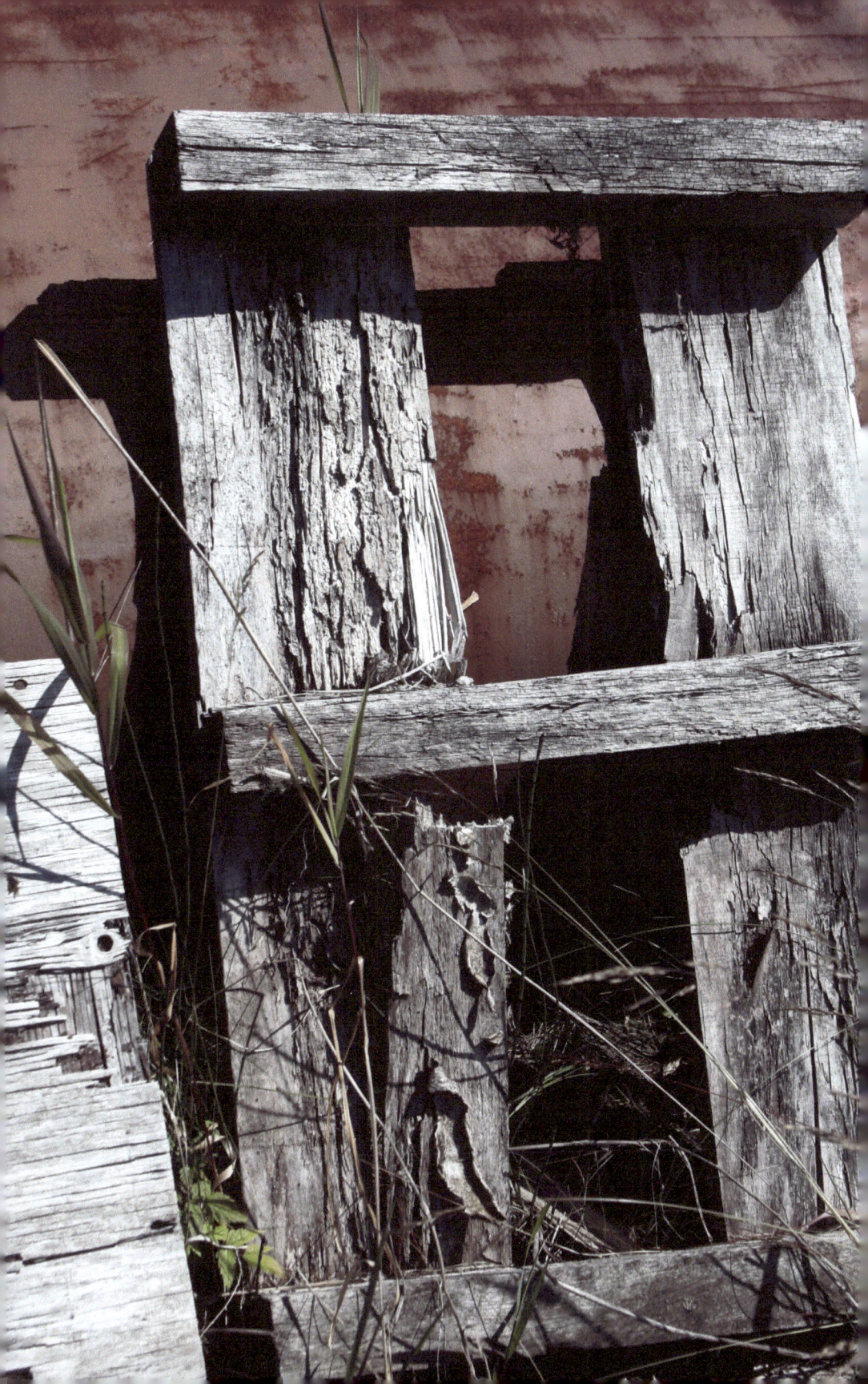

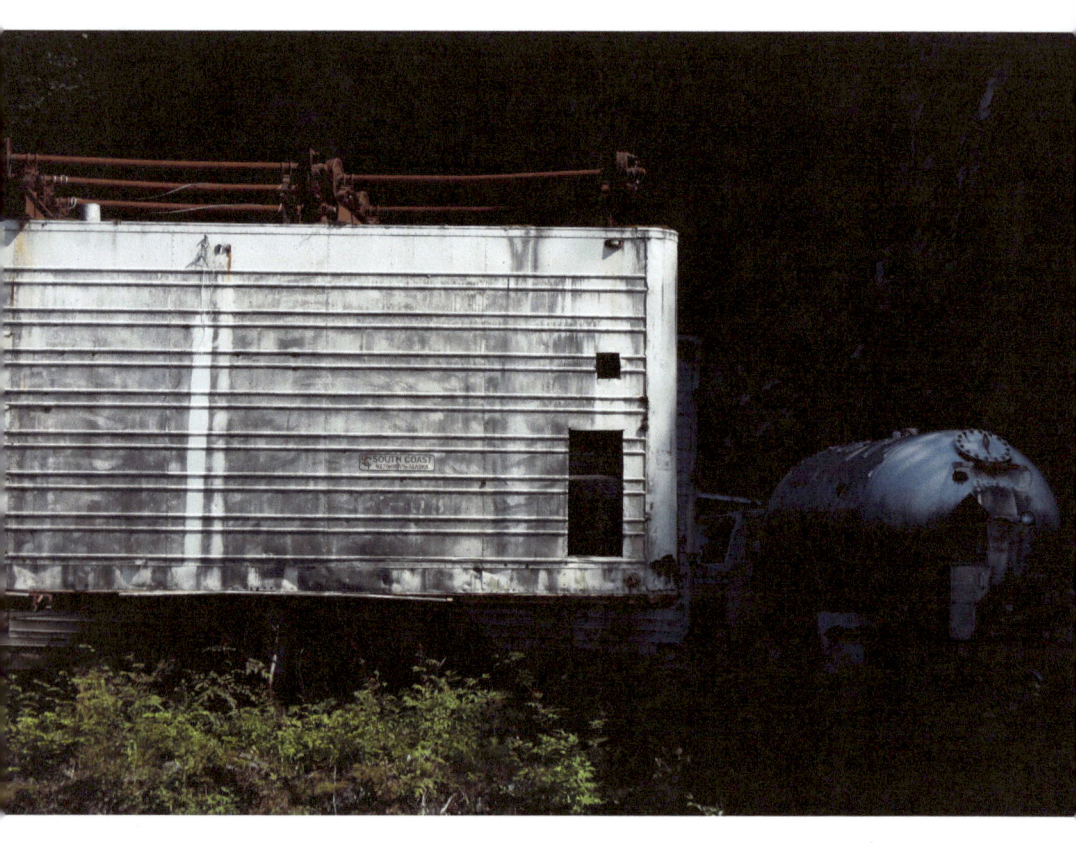

Taking a big sip, she continued. "Listen, Amanda. The closer you get to a miracle, the more your doubts will increase. Sometimes you can even use doubts as a way to predict how close you are. If you're having way more doubts than normal, you're getting closer."

Amanda looked at her. "Last night I dreamed my plant lit the fire that burned our house," she said.

Amanda's grandmother considered that. "Dreams aren't always true," she said. "What else happened in your dream?"

"The plant turned into my angry neighbor. He was laughing while the house burned."

"Well, *that* part was probably true – the part about your neighbor being glad your house burned."

"He won't stay glad," said Amanda's grandfather.

He had silently walked up and joined them without Amanda even noticing he had arrived. He poured himself a lemonade.

"Great spot," he said to Amanda's grandmother. "I like being between the watermelons and pumpkins."

"It's become my favorite spot, too," she said.

"Your neighbor," said Amanda's grandfather, "will be happy for a short while, glad he got you out of the neighborhood. But he won't be happy long. People never get a victory they can enjoy by being cruel or mean or laughing at someone's distress.

"Anyway," he said brightening, "You don't have to worry about him. If you keep getting better at porcelain, you've got a great career ahead of you. I saw the bridge and rainbow. Magnificent! The best you've done so far – maybe the best porcelain I've *ever* seen. And, if you keep at it, I'm confident you'll improve even more. There's no telling how far you'll go. But you'll have to push your doubts aside. Sometimes your doubts will keep you from realizing how good your work is."

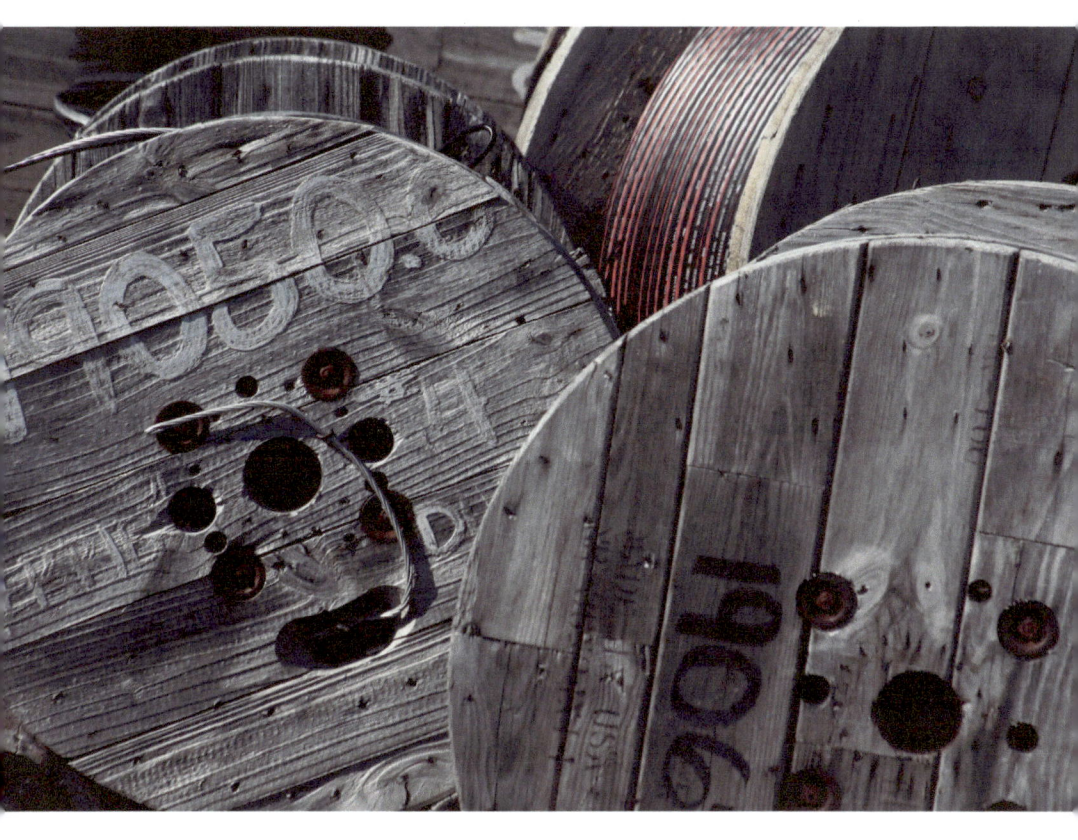

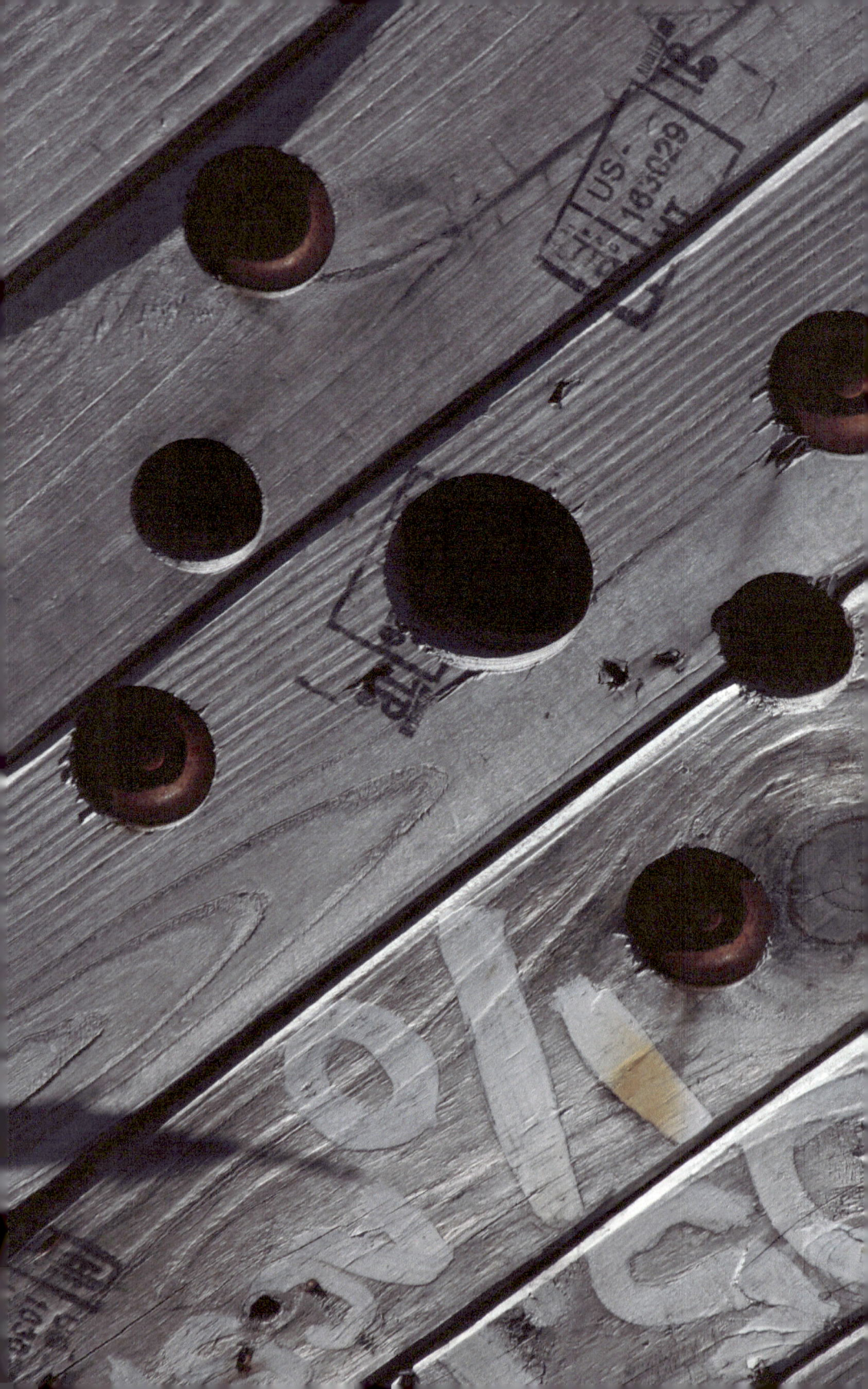

"Mom doesn't think the porcelain matters," said Amanda.

"Well, that's not *quite* true," said Amanda's grandmother. "She likes anything you're interested in. But you're right that she doesn't think the porcelain can help your plants. And she's not sure where you get the figurines."

"I could show her," said Amanda.

Amanda's grandfather and grandmother both laughed at the same time.

"I don't think that would work out too well," said her grandmother. "Your mom still doesn't believe I can pull pumpkins out of the air."

"I could tell her I saw you do it."

"No, dear. She'd just think you were telling fibs. The fact is, she has seen me pull them out of the air several times herself, and she *still* doesn't think I can do it. She just thinks I'm good at tricking her."

"Amanda," said her grandfather, "you should know that not everybody will like you to do miracles. Your neighbor hated it. Your mom probably won't believe it, even when she sees it. But some people will be cheering you on. Your grandmother and I will, for sure.

"Anyway, I came out to the garden because I wanted to tell you something: You're getting quite good, Amanda. Stick with it, even when you have doubts. After you get your first miracle, there's always more."

He turned to Amanda's grandmother. "Thanks for the lemonade," he said. "It's good to have you here. You should show Amanda her part of the garden." Then he walked back to the house, stopwatch in hand.

A few minutes earlier, Amanda hadn't been sure she *wanted* to see her part of the garden. She had thought about ripping her plants out and maybe even smashing the porcelain. But, holding her grandmother's hand, she went out to look.

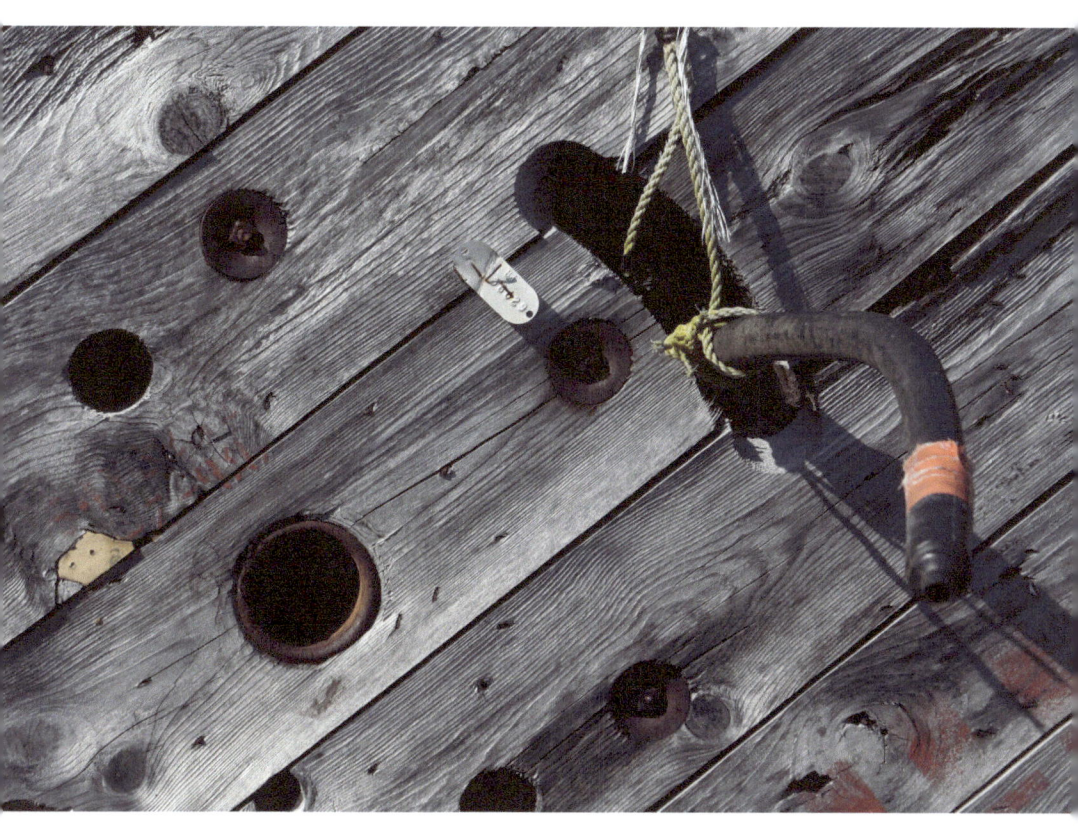

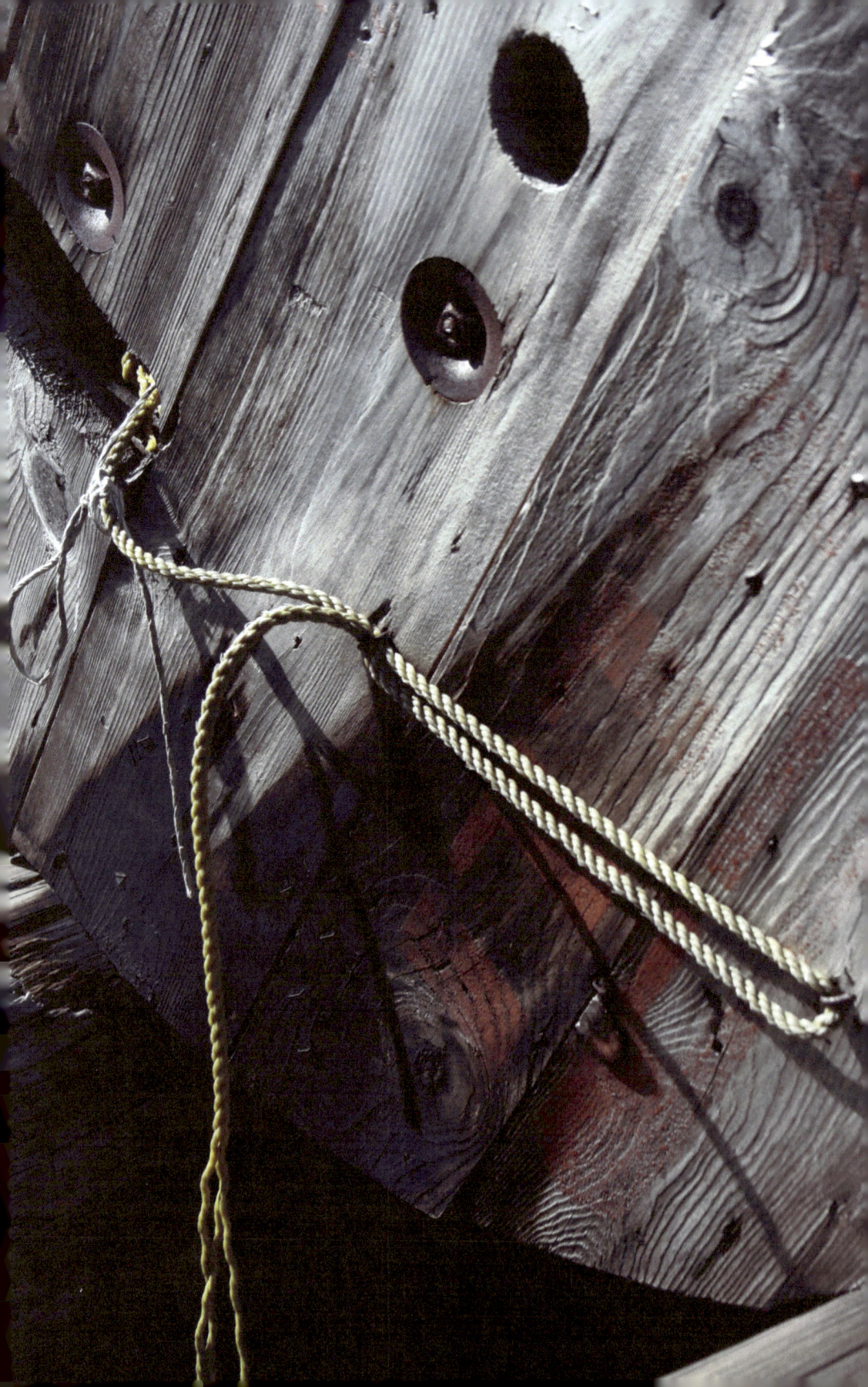

Meanwhile, in Amanda's old neighborhood, the neighbor next to Amanda's burned house was scowling even more than normal. His face was as purple as an eggplant and he was as angry as he ever got.

He had thought he would be happy when he set fire to Amanda's fence. But now that the fence was gone, he had a clear view of her garden. Every time he glanced out his window he could see how well Amanda's plants were recovering from his attempts to destroy them. Plus, with the fence gone *everyone* in the neighborhood had a clear view of how beautiful the plants were. People were starting to walk over to admire them, and the news of their beauty and fragrance was spreading fast. The previous night he had noticed two neighbors sneaking into Amanda's garden to get cuttings of the plants to take to their own homes. Soon the whole neighborhood was going to be transformed. And not in the way he had hoped.

The worst, he thought, was that with the fence gone everyone in the neighborhood would see if he tried to hurt the plants one more time. He scowled and sneezed. He didn't know what to do.

When Amanda got to her part of her grandfather's garden, she saw that the four shoots had each started budding. Two already had flowers. The air was thick with fragrance. But the biggest surprise was in the center of the shoots, where Amanda had planted the enormous seed with the green glop.

Amanda gasped. She had expected a plant to grow from that seed. But instead, there was her miracle. The one she had hoped and longed for. The one she had worked to get for almost a year.

Amanda blinked. She couldn't believe it. How could it have appeared overnight? How could it have been so easy? Was it really there?

She blinked again. Her miracle didn't disappear. The miracle Amanda had been hoping for (and for so long!) was right before her eyes.

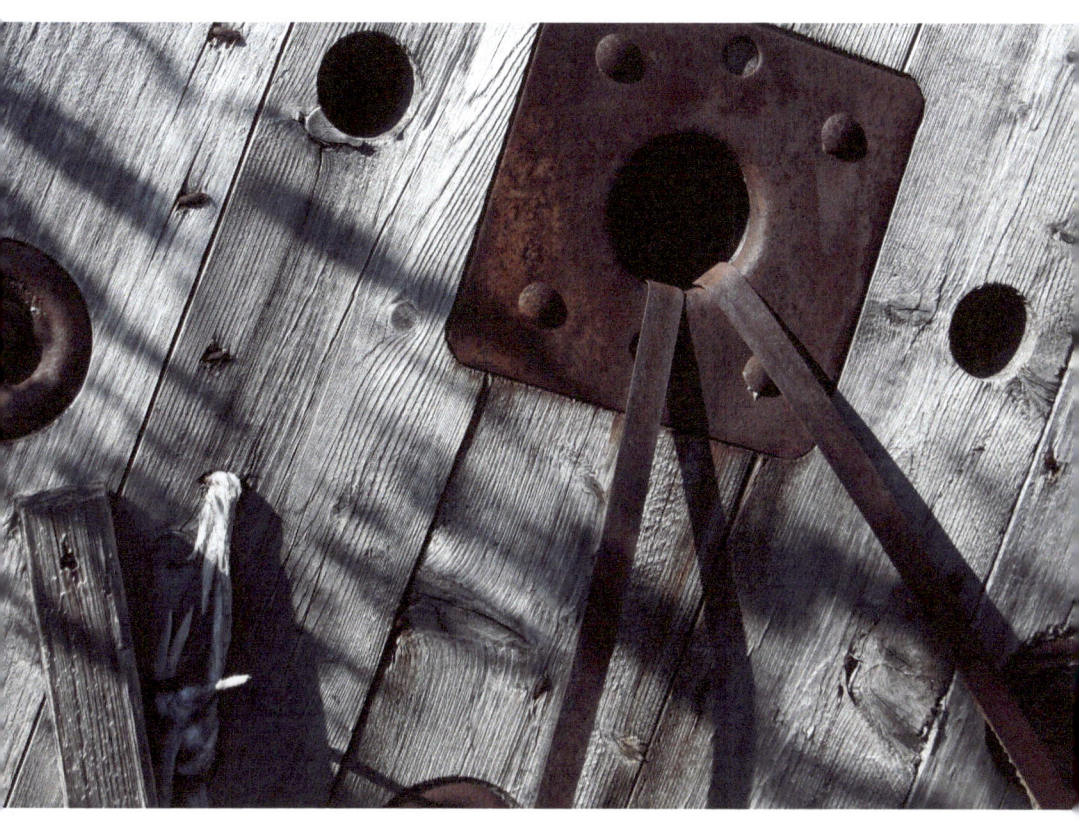

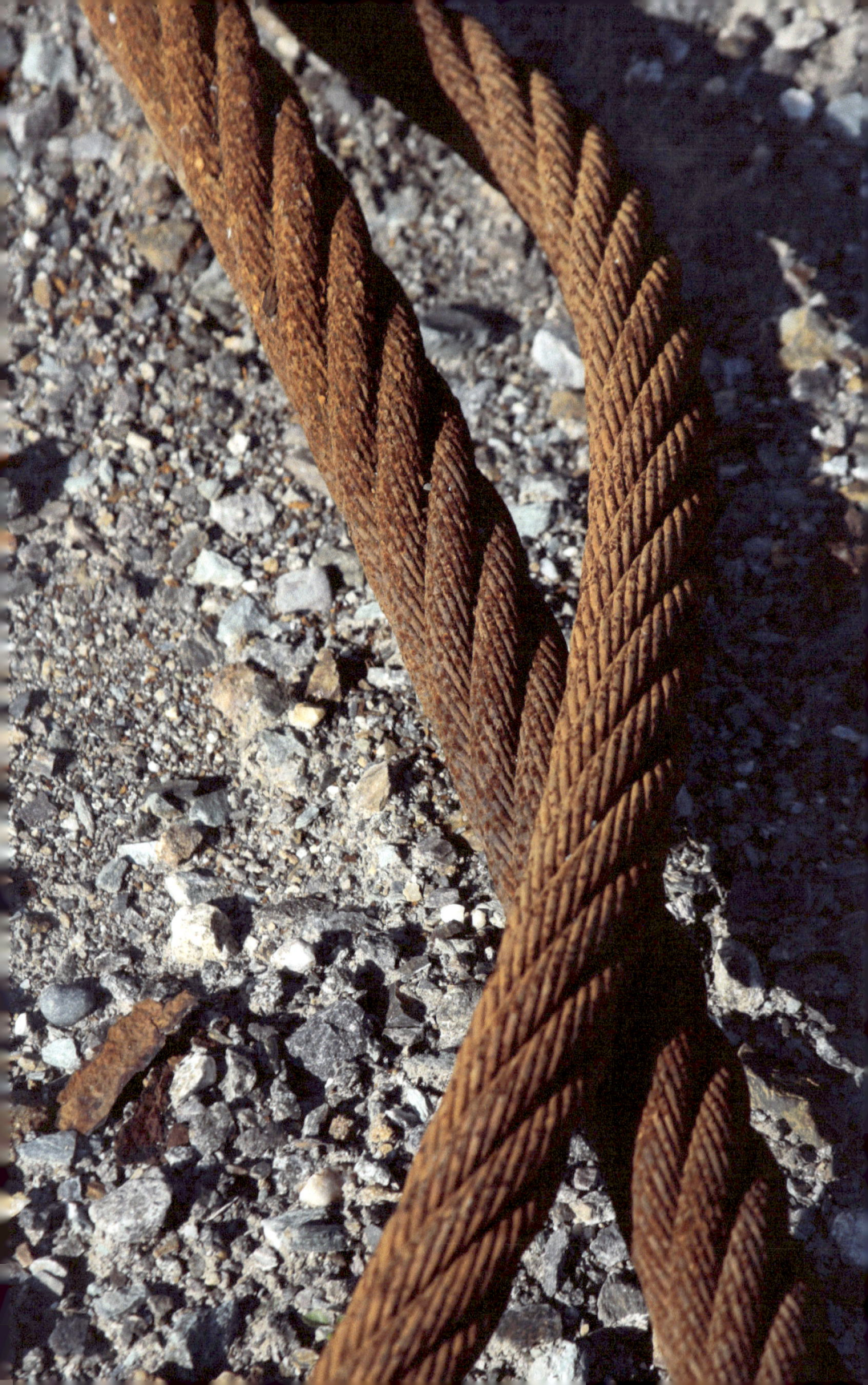

Amanda's grandmother was so delighted she pulled a pumpkin out of the air just for fun. Then she put it back and got a watermelon instead. She and Amanda celebrated by eating thick slices.

Half way through her first piece of watermelon, Amanda realized she knew exactly what she wanted to do next. But she didn't say. At least not yet.

~~

Reflection questions

People can have doubts even when they are doing something great. What do *you* do when *you* have doubts? (Do you quit? Keep going? Do doubts change your attitude?)

Some people will oppose you even if you are doing something good. How do you respond when people don't appreciate what you are doing?

Amanda got her miracle. What great things have you gotten?

What are you still waiting for?

What are you doing to pull those things out of the air?

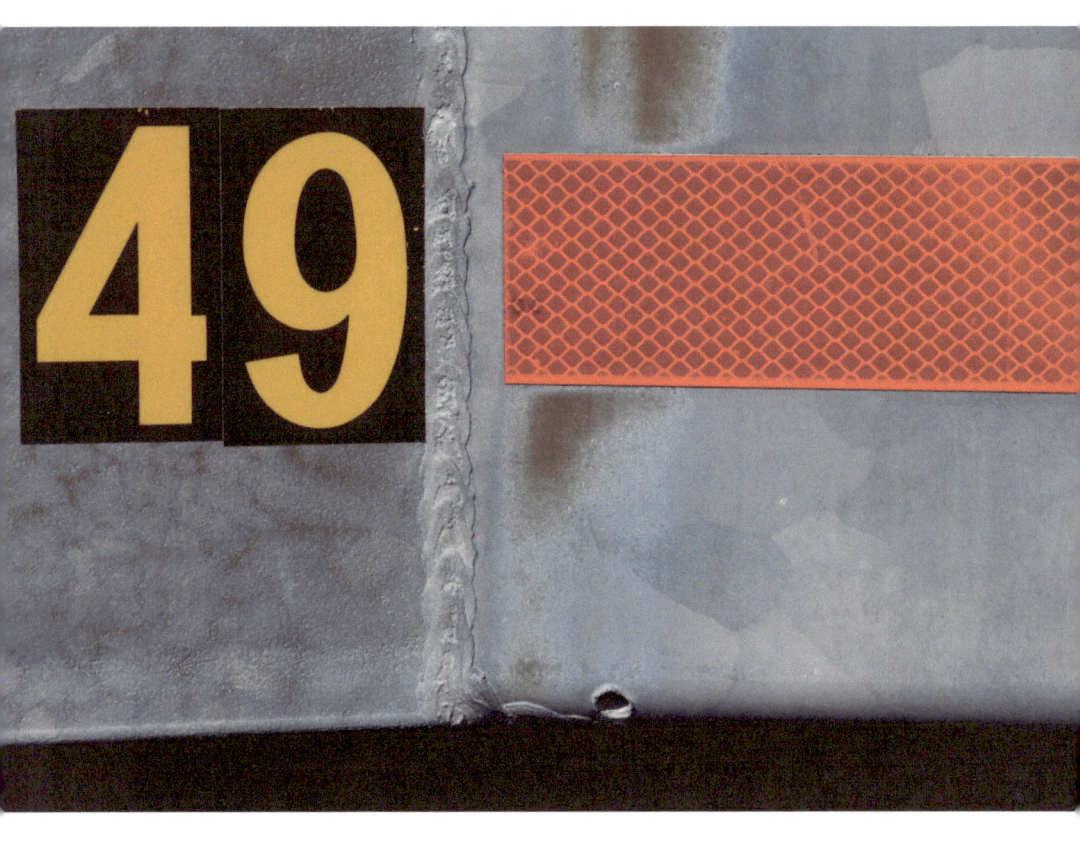

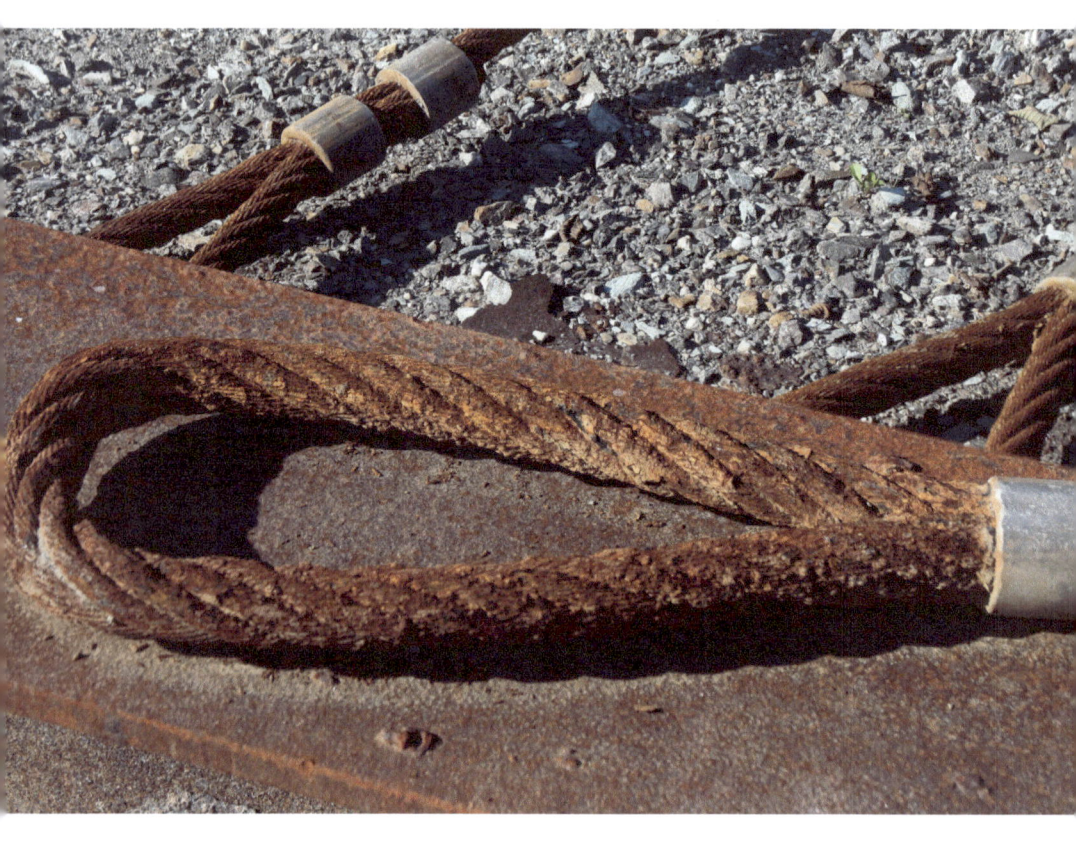

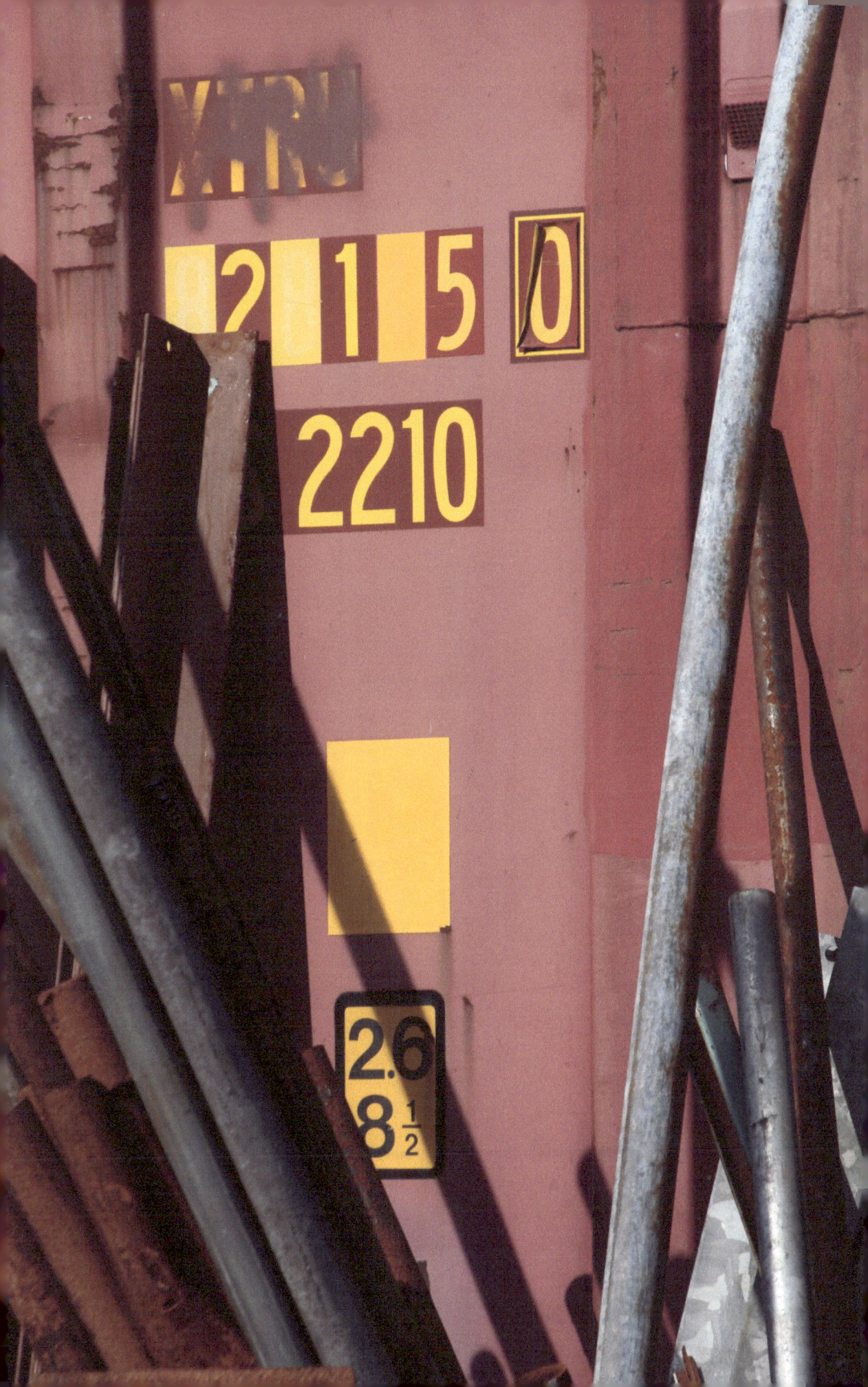

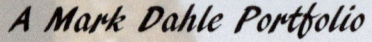

A Mark Dahle Portfolio

Farmer Jane

This Mark Dahle Portfolio includes a beautiful painting, twenty-five gorgeous photographs from the Netherlands, and a story about Farmer Jane.

Jane didn't know that farmers have troubles.

But she was about to discover how *many* troubles they have.

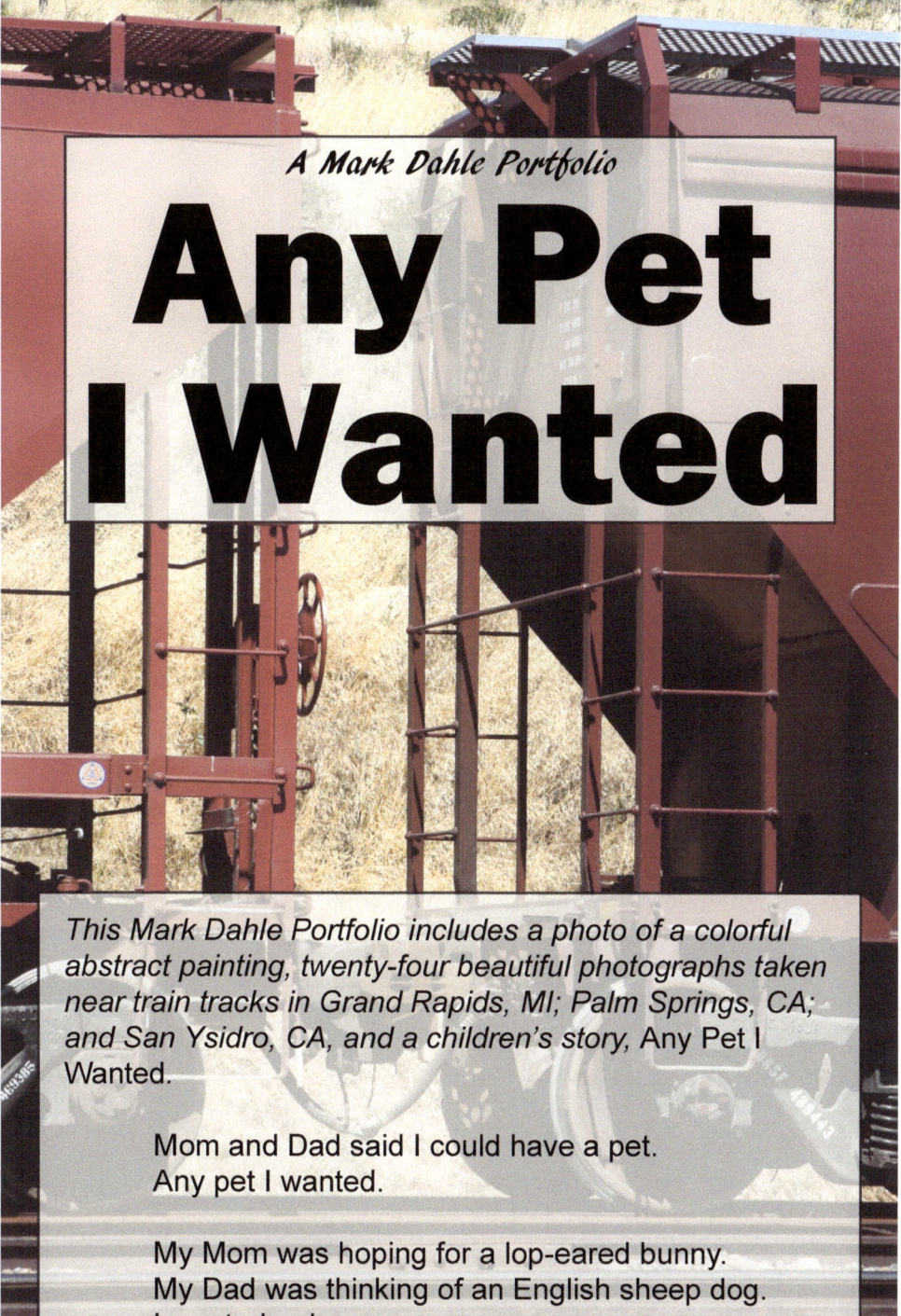

A Mark Dahle Portfolio

Any Pet I Wanted

This Mark Dahle Portfolio includes a photo of a colorful abstract painting, twenty-four beautiful photographs taken near train tracks in Grand Rapids, MI; Palm Springs, CA; and San Ysidro, CA, and a children's story, Any Pet I Wanted.

Mom and Dad said I could have a pet.
Any pet I wanted.

My Mom was hoping for a lop-eared bunny.
My Dad was thinking of an English sheep dog.
I wanted a dragon.

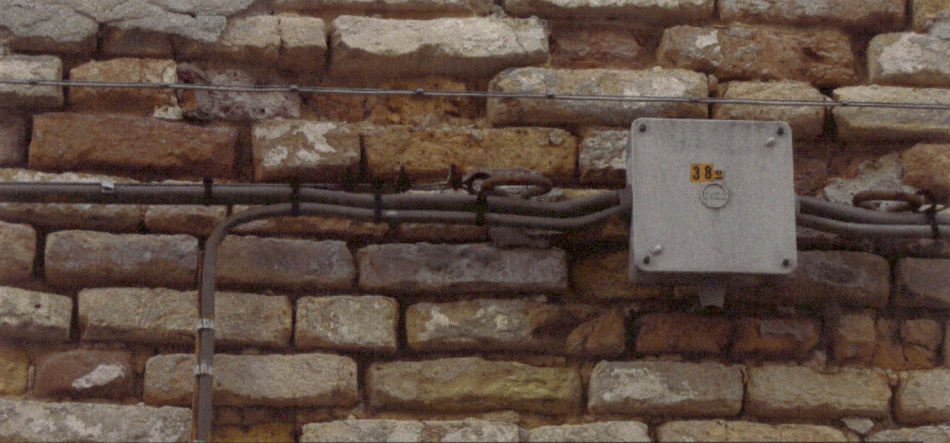

A Mark Portfolio

The Boy Who Loved Monopoly

This Mark Dahle Portfolio includes a colorful painting, twenty-seven beautiful photographs of Venice, and a story about a boy who loved to play Monopoly. One day the boy received $250,000 as an inheritance.

You probably haven't inherited any money this week.
But you've got lots of gifts
and lots of things that you're good at —
or could be, after you get more practice.
What will *you* do with all the gifts that *you* have?